With the Saraguros

With the Saraguros

THE BLENDED LIFE IN A
TRANSNATIONAL WORLD

David Syring

University of Texas Press   *Austin*

"Why Log Truck Drivers Rise Earlier Than Students of Zen," from
No Nature, by Gary Snyder, copyright © 1992 by Gary Snyder. Used
by permission of Pantheon Books, an imprint of the Knopf Doubleday
Publishing Group, a division of Random House LLC. All rights reserved.

"Tales from the Exotics Battlefront: Four Stories of Exotics Gone Awry,"
by Natasha Kassulke, from *Wisconsin Natural Resources Magazine* © 2001.
Used by permission.

Requests for permission to reproduce material from this work should be
sent to:
    Permissions
    University of Texas Press
    P.O. Box 7819
    Austin, TX 78713-7819
    http://utpress.utexas.edu/index.php/rp-form

⊗ The paper used in this book meets the minimum requirements of
ANSI/NISO Z39.48-1992 (R1997) (Permanence of Paper).

LIBRARY OF CONGRESS CATALOGING-IN-PUBLICATION DATA
Syring, David, 1967–
    With the Saraguros : the blended life in a transnational world /
David Syring.
        pages   cm
    Includes bibliographical references and index.
    ISBN 978-0-292-76093-6 (hardback)
1. Saraguro Indians—Social life and customs   2. Saraguro Indians—
Ethnic identity.   3. Saraguro Region (Ecuador)—Social life and customs.
4. Globalization—Social aspects—Ecuador—Saraguro Region.   I. Title.
    F3722.1.S37S97   2014
    986.6—dc23   2014015483

doi:10.7560/760936

Dedicated to the people of Saraguro, especially
Ana Victoria Sarango and Manuel Benigno Cango,
whose good lives and good will inspire me.

And for Mitra, Selene, and Roshan, who are the
root of my good life.

*Dedicado a la gente de Saraguro, especialmente
Ana Victoria Sarango y Manuel Benigno Cango,
cuya vida buena y voluntad buena me inspiran.*

*Y para Mitra, Selene y Roshan, quienes son las
raíces de mi vida buena.*

Contents

Acknowledgments

WITHOUT MY FIRST, BEST READER, MITRA EMAD, I would have a messier and much less interesting set of ideas to share. Her intellect and compassionate heart fills this book and my life with more energy than I could ever have generated alone.

This book would not have been possible without the introduction to Saraguro generously provided to me, both in person and through their scholarly work, by Linda and Jim Belote. My gratitude to them grows with each year that passes and deepens my connections with Benigno, Ana Victoria, and the other Saraguros I have the good fortune to call friends.

Two articles I wrote that were published by the journal *Anthropology and Humanism*, "*La Vida Matizada*: Time Sense, Everyday Rhythms, and Globalized Ideas of Work" [December 2009] and "Sweet Water and Exotic Fish: Ethnographic Reflections of Environmental Imaginations in Ecuador and the Great Lakes" [June 2007]), helped me sprout the seeds that have grown into this work. I am grateful to Edie Turner for supporting my writing efforts. Theresa May, at the University of Texas Press, has been a supporter of this and my previous book, and I thank her for her encouragement. Andrea Heckman, first through the inspiration provided by her remarkable book, *Woven Stories*, and later through her supportive and perceptive comments on my manuscript, improved this book immensely. My colleague at the University of Minnesota Duluth, Tim Roufs, also provided valuable feedback, as did an anonymous reviewer for the University of Texas Press.

Funding provided by the University of Minnesota Duluth College of Liberal Arts and by the McKnight Foundation Imagine Grant program has allowed me to travel regularly to Saraguro.

With the Saraguros

Prologue

ADVICE TO A TECHNOPELLI

Check all the pockets.

Not everybody likes your music,
  or your visit to this place.
    You're welcome in many places in the community—
     But not here!
     Or not now!

Tractor time costs more—
  you can wait—
    watch, maybe you'll learn something,
     and pitch in if they'll let you.

Sometimes there are only three stones
  firm in the muddy path—step carefully.

People will ask for your help—
  give as much as you can—
    don't promise to change lives—
     know your true worth and limits as a traveler.

Sometimes your technology won't work.
  Sometimes your technology won't be appreciated.
    Sometimes your technology will be useful to people you visit.
    Be aware of when each of these appears true.
    Act accordingly.

Most of the places you walk in your adventures
        are walked daily by four-year-olds.

Sweet treats in your pockets
        are always welcome.

Kids can be helpful guides, but remember,
        they don't know all the houses.
                (they do know the location of all bad dogs.)

Dogs, horses, sheep and some people
        don't really much like strangers,
                cows basically don't care.

For dogs, a stone in your hand
        can be useful.

Bring everything inside you,
        not just your brain —
                and use it all, every day.
                        You're first human,
                                traveler second.

Women standing at the top of the cliff path,
        having their morning chat while hand-spinning wool,
                do not want you to take their picture. Don't ask.

Young men of the community might keep their distance —
        they have their reasons.

Old men will ask questions you can't answer
        about why your country is wealthier than theirs.
                Old women who have never worn shoes
                        will probably not talk to you —
                                there's a good chance they do not speak
                                        the same language as others in the
                                        community.

People will tell you a certain old woman
        is more than one hundred years old —
                this may or may not be true.

Morning yoga is a good way to keep mental balance while
journeying.
        Good idea to keep it up back home.

Folks at home want a polished and edited
        version of your story.

The stories need to be (mostly) true,
        and carefully told—
            honor the trust of those you visit.

Wash your shoes before you go home.

VISITING THE *PUCARÁ*

Field notes, August 15, 2009: We have been sitting for hours,
beading. Late in the afternoon, after I have finished the last row of the
fresas (strawberries) model necklace I have been working on since Mon-
day when Aleja got me started, Benigno says he wants to take me for a
walk to the *pucará*. He has been working steadily on necklaces, too. He
helps Ana Victoria as she scrambles to finish a bunch of pieces for me to
take back to the States to sell.

So we set out for a sweet, final walk for this trip, down the road to Tio
Loma, past the new volleyball *cancha* for that sector of Tuncarta. We walk
at first in amiable silence, but as we get closer to a high hill visible from
all over Tuncarta, Benigno explains the concept of the *pucará*, a community's sacred spot, where important gatherings and fiestas are supposed to
be held. Every community is supposed to have a high spot from which it
is possible to see every house in the community and that is visible from
every house. He says this tradition dates back to the Incas. (Later I find
that *pucará*—from the Quichua word for "fortress"—is a term commonly
used throughout the Andes to refer to Incan, and sometimes pre-Incan,
ruins.) Tuncarta's *pucará*, located just above a field that Ana Victoria inherited from her father, offers a wonderful spot from which to view the
surrounding terrain.

Benigno points out a few flaws in the way the site has been developed.
To one side a plantation of pines and eucalyptus trees blocks the view of
part of the community. He thinks these should be removed to keep the
sacred spot visible to all. In addition, in 1984, some young people built a
cement slab on the *pucará*.

"That shouldn't be here," he says. "It isn't proper to have cement in a sacred place."

He points out a very high hill across the river. It is a hill I have often wondered about as I have looked at it from the window of my room. A nearly vertical planting of corn leads up one slope to its flat top. Benigno says that spot is the *pucará* for Gurudel—the community that lies below. He has some stake in that community, as his Hierba Buena farm, containing most of his inherited land, lies there. A large, antique olla, or jar, that he showed me a few weeks ago comes from that spot.

"The slopes of the Gurudel *pucará* are covered with old pottery, probably from the Incas," he says.

"This *pucará*," he says, as he gestures to the hill we stand on, "This one used to have pottery shards everywhere, too, but people have been taking them over the years, and they are scarce now."

He says the Gurudel *pucará* is much higher and remote, so people go there less frequently for purposes outside of ritual gatherings.

Benigno says Tuncarta, Oñacapac, Lagunas, Gurudel, and a few other communities have *pucarás*, but not all the rural communities do.

"It's something important and historical," he says.

As we climb down the hill, Benigno calls to an older man who is walking on the road, "Hello, Uncle, do you have any cheese?"

"No, I don't," calls the man.

"Any *huajango*?" Benigno calls.

"No, that neither."

We walk down to the road, the same direction as the man. Benigno says he wants to check whether another woman has either *huajango* (a lightly fermented agave beverage) or cheese, but when we get to her house, she isn't home. The man Benigno called Uncle comes over from his nearby house, and we exchange greetings. Benigno explains that the man is Ana Victoria's uncle.

"He weaves beautiful ponchos," Benigno says.

We go to see his loom, a four-pedal harness model, that fills a third of the adobe house the man shares with his wife. He is working on a long bolt of dark brown cloth of undyed sheep's wool. He calls this color *negro*, black. The weave—a tight, twilled pattern requiring a complicated set of steps on the four pedals—feels rich to the touch. He shows us a few passes of his shuttle and adjusts the loom to let out more warp thread. The loom is old and well used. Benigno admires the heddle made with bamboo slats—it is wide enough to weave a piece of fabric almost two yards across. I take some video of the man weaving.

"Will you show me how to do this?" Benigno asks about the technique.

The man rises and Benigno sits to try a few rows with the shuttle.

"I'd like to learn to make a heddle like this," Benigno says. "So you can teach me how to weave well."

The man's wife shows a fine, completed poncho. Benigno looks stylish as he tries it on.

"It would be good for keeping warm while riding my motorcycle at night," he says.

The house teems with baskets full of yarn.

"Do you spin all of the yarn he uses to weave with?" I ask.

She smiles and nods. During her lifetime she has made miles of fine handspun.

We take our leave and head up the hill, stopping to visit at the house of Ana Victoria's maternal grandmother. Then as Benigno and I walk up the hill below his house, we pass an old stone oven in the twilight—a relic once used to make lime for plastering adobe houses.

Benigno says the place has also been a spot of gathering energies, positive and negative. And then he tells a story that he says is true, not a fictional *cuento*, or tale.

"About twenty years ago, a teenage girl—someone I went to school with—was walking home from a fiesta around 11 p.m. or later when she passed this oven in the darkness," he begins. "As she passed by, she felt two hands pressing down on her shoulders from behind, but when she turned, no one was there. The next day she grew ill. Within eight days she died. I visited her while she was sick. She was curled up, unable to move from a fetal position."

He doesn't say the weight of the ghostly hands on her shoulders killed her, rather that the *mal aire* she got that night killed her. A bit later, as I am writing in my notepad, I explain that I am recording the *cuento* of the girl. Benigno insists it is not a fiction, but reality—he knew the girl and saw her before she died—again reaffirming a distinction he has made before, between a *cuento*—something like a fable—and a real event told as a story.

As we climb the last hundred yards of the hill, Benigno stops to show a plant he calls *allichilchi*, an eight-foot shrub with small yellow flowers.

"This is good for *mal aire*," he says and pulls off a short branch. "And for *susto*, especially if you are frightened by an animal."

He swats me gently on my legs and body to show how to use the plant, and I am surrounded by a medicinal, somewhat acrid but not unpleasant odor as the leaves and flowers release their volatile oils.

"So much more to learn," I say as we continue up the hill. "There's always so much more to learn."

Benigno nods.

"Because the old people never write, and never wrote, anything down," he says. "I write a little bit down, but there is always more to learn from the old people."

I nod, too—seems there will always be work in this town for a technopelli.

WHAT IT MEANS TO BE A TECHNOPELLI

Here is a discovery I made about the traveling storyteller Kokopelli while walking through the Otavalo market in Cuenca. One vendor offered a shirt with an embroidered Kokopelli design stitched on the chest. When I asked why he is using an image that comes from one of the native groups of my country, he insisted that the image originated in the Oriente (the Ecuadorian term referring to the Amazon basin—located in the eastern part of the country).

Kokopelli first appears in cultures far to the north of Ecuador. So this Otavalo merchant's claim seems thin, but it is a nice irony that the Otavalos are using Kokopelli's image in their products. Otavalo is a center of weaving in Ecuador, and the Otavalos have long been known as shrewd traders and commercial agents. Otavalos travel all over the world, and they often make their livings by selling weavings and playing folk music. If you see performers wearing ponchos and hats and playing Andean music at folk festivals or in big cities, there is a pretty good chance they are Otavalos.

According to one theory, Kokopelli, the humpbacked flute player common throughout the American Southwest, represents a historical pattern of lone travelers walking long distances to trade. The hump on his back represents a pack full of seeds (according to the Tohono O'odham people of the Sonoran Desert) and trade goods. Kokopelli traveled, played songs, and swapped stories with the people he met. As a metaphoric figure, he combines the wanderings of Odysseus, the talents of a traveling salesman, and the tale telling of a griot. Here is a description of this theory as reported by Sharman Apt Russell in *Songs of the Flute Player: Seasons of Life in the Southwest*:

> Most archeologists agree that Kokopelli "diffused upward" from the south to northern Mexico and the American Southwest. In this spread of culture, a main source of influence was the *pochteca* or trader: a solitary merchant who traveled up and down the continent exchanging goods such as macaws, shells, pyrite mirrors, peyote, slaves, and turquoise. In the *pochteca* theory, the hump on Koko-

pelli's back is actually a pack of goods, and one botanist has suggested that the Quichua Indians of the Andes are the specific ancestors of Kokopelli. Evidence of this lies in plant genetics. Ancient ears of a pod corn found in Arizona ruins are similar to a relic corn commonly stocked by Bolivian medicine men; in the mid-twentieth century, these merchants were still traveling through Central and South America playing their traditional reed flute, carrying a small blanket-pack, selling the corn as a cure for respiratory problems. (1991, 38)

Kokopelli has long been a compelling figure to me; one of the earliest necklaces I made—years before I met and began to work with Saraguro beadworkers—has a Kokopelli worked into it. I seriously considered writing my dissertation on "genetic erosion" in food seedstocks caused by increasing corporate control over our food systems. Years ago I wrote the beginning of a novel set not too far in the future, when corporations control the seedstock of plants, raising your own food is illegal, and the people who violate corporate patent laws to make that possible are "kokopellis," travelers who carry open-pollinated seeds across the borders of corporate states. I never finished the novel, but the image of a kokopelli carrying seeds and good will, and trying to build community wherever he or she travels, has stuck with me.

So, considering the theory that Kokopelli's hump is a pack of trade goods and he is a traveling salesman/musician/storyteller who is a Quichua-speaking Indian from the Andes, the fact that Otavalos are selling his image now has a nice kind of symmetry—a reversal of the history of an icon.

Kokopelli's travels offer a useful metaphor for the work of an anthropologist. When I travel to Ecuador, I bring a few packets of seeds (most recently sunflowers, as requested by Mami Petrona, Benigno's mother), songs, and stories. Given that I also bring technologies such as HD cameras and digital voice recorders, I have come to think of the anthropologist's role as a *technopelli*. One of an anthropologist's primary tasks is to listen to and gather stories about life in various parts of the world and share them with our communities, our students, and readers in our own countries and beyond. I also see the technopelli's role as bringing the tools used in teaching and research to assist the communities we work with in whatever ways they see as valuable to them. When I visit Saraguro, people want to know about life in my place, so I also carry stories from my home place to the places I visit. I help them make films of their craftwork and dancing. Perhaps this small exchange helps make new kinds of globalization-from-below that serve human interests instead of globalization-from-above serving primarily the interests of capital and the elites who control it?

One of the nicknames I have been given by Ana Victoria, my beading teacher in Saraguro, is "un hombre de muchas cosas"—a man of many things. It would be nice to think she means that I am sophisticated and resourceful, like James Bond, but I think she means I have a lot of stuff. I carry a whole mindset and system of technologies into her daily life, and we explore together how best to use them to generate mutual understanding. By these small steps toward cross-cultural understanding, I contribute my work and voice to a more holistically connected world where people treasure their own places, as well as the stories and places of others.

CHAPTER ONE

Attuning and the Development
of an Approach to Fieldwork

WHERE ARE THE SOUNDS OF THE FROGS CREAKING in the puddles and trees around Ana Victoria's house on a wet night or the roosters crowing at all odd hours? Where are the smells of the eucalyptus trees in the breeze or the plantains and empanadas spattering in the hot grease? Where are the nearly daily glimpses of rainbows and double rainbows manifesting in the damp *paramo* winds off the mountains? What about the constant company of the news or *musica nacional* from the radio that is always on? Or regular bursts of laughter from the beading table on the porch as the kids swirl through the yard in their games? The encouragements of "Tuki, tuki!" ("toucan! toucan!") as the shy youngest one tries to keep up? Where are the continuous queries of "A ver?" as yet another kid from the neighborhood stands on the road above the house holding a dime, seeking the sweet *chupetis* that Ana Victoria sells from her one-room store?

Any attempt to represent experience in written words is destined to be only a shadow of reality. There is much I do not know or have not been able to convey about my Saraguro friends and their local and transnational lives—in fact, the old adage "The more you learn, the less you know" is too appropriate here. However, this book offers a glimpse into the lives of an indigenous group, the Saraguros of the Andean highlands of southern Ecuador, as well as a meditation on the anthropological project of cross-cultural understanding. Rather than depict the Saraguros as an isolated, bounded ethnic community, this book explores how cultural identities interpenetrate, blur, and blend, both for indigenous peoples and for the anthropologists who work with them in the contemporary world.

Much of what I write here does not seek explicitly to analyze and interpret; rather, it strives to evoke—both the lives of my Saraguro friends and my own experiences as an anthropologist. This emphasis on experience over exegesis is both a deliberate strategy and an acknowledgment of the limitations and partiality of what I know. I have been visiting Saraguro for four to six weeks one or two times a year for the last eight years. This seems to be enough time to say some interesting things about the experience but insufficient time to claim interpretive prerogative. This book tells the stories of someone who pays close attention in Saraguro, but only during those brief periods of time when I can balance my personal life as a husband and father with my professional life as anthropologist and teacher. In fact, the balancing and blending of these roles corresponds to *la vida matizada*, the blended life, that my Saraguro friends have helped me to see and develop.

Anthropology describes many crucial relationships between individuals from different societies as a key means for cultural understanding. This was especially so in the second half of the twentieth century. Examples include Marjorie Shostak and Nisa (Shostak 1981), Paul Stoller and Adamu Jenitongo (Stoller and Olkes 1989; Stoller 2005), Ruth Behar and Esperanza (Behar 1993), Vincent Crapanzano and Tuhami (Crapanzano 1980), Karen Brown and Mama Lola (Alourdes; see Brown 1991), and the list could go on. These are a few relevant characters in the storybook of anthropology: The anthropologist and the key interlocutor. The storyteller and the story listener. Community member and traveling technopelli. This complementary pair is part of the basic substance out of which qualitative anthropology emerges and enters into the collective consciousness of the world. In this book, "Benigno" and "David" are two more of these characters, talking to one another, showing one another places, telling one another stories.

Fieldwork uproots a person from daily life and requires a kind of attuning. "To attune" seems an appropriate verb for the process out of which anthropological engagements arise. To tune is to bring an instrument into the right pitch to make a particular piece of music. To attune for fieldwork is to set one's consciousness to be open and receptive and ready to engage with the types of emotional and intellectual encounters that make up anthropological fieldwork. It feels like taking a guitar that is set to one tuning—the one required to live one's usual, everyday life—and re-tensioning the strings in order to live a different kind of life—one that settles into daily rhythms set by conditions in a cultural setting other than one's own. Adjusting to different daily rhythms—that is the core of an anthropological consciousness, learning in your body and being that there are many ways to live in time, all of them inflected by cultures and the ideas they put into our minds.

The role of anthropological observer comes easily to me. Watching and participating and being mostly silent while people talk or do or show how to do things — relishing the ambiguity of understanding only part of what is being said or done while following the main gist of the conversation or action — these are part of the negative capability that keeps attention focused and full of the questioning attunement needed to explore why people do things the way they do.

My first project and book (Syring 2000), the graduate school research for which I earned my professional credentials, was not in an exotic other society; it was in my home culture. Owing to my temperament and interests and an intellectually stimulating and creatively supportive atmosphere cultivated in the 1990s at Rice University by George Marcus, Michael Fischer, Steven Tyler, Sharon Traweek, and others, I did not follow the model laid down by many of our anthropological ancestors. Not only did I do my first fieldwork in my own country — the United States — I did it in one of the places of my home identity: the Texas Hill Country. This is the place where my German ancestors settled in the mid-1800s and where many in my extended family still live. The history of my family in Texas is not a simple one, and part of the reason I set out on that path was to explore the legacies of abuse and poverty that have shaped the region and my own personal history. I went to the Hill Country to understand the historical and cultural contexts that led my father to become an alcoholic and abuser.

What I found was a large extended family that has made itself into a creative community of mutual support and affection while remaining uneven on an economic level. Some of my father's twelve brothers and sisters have had successful professional lives, while others have struggled with poverty. The bond that holds them together is storytelling of all kinds. I was fascinated to discover the contours of that bond and to see that histories of abuse and poverty result in very different lives, even for people from the same family. My first book (Syring 2000) explored this cultural context and looked at how Hill Country residents have used its distinctive history, and the built and natural environment, to create what is now the region's primary economic engine — cultural and natural tourism. In an interesting parallel, many of my Saraguro friends talk about trying to make similar heritage and natural tourism ventures in hopes of creating economic opportunity for their families.

Creating that book taught me many lessons on writing about people and culture. Here is a visceral lesson that I feel as much as think: the people you work with in anthropological research are real people, not cultural ciphers to be decoded. When you sit down with a woman who has suffered from diabetes for most of her life, has had a double mastectomy, and has not had life opportunities such as a good education or a supportive family, and when that woman is your aunt and tells stories about your own childhood and the childhood of your father and feeds you sausage and *pannis* and sweet iced tea, you know that you can't write about her participation in charismatic religious healing as if it were some odd cultural adaptation. Anything you write has to attempt to represent her as a real human being, with the dignity and foibles of any human being. To do less would be personally troubling and, more, ethically wrong. My approach to writing anthropology has been deeply shaped by the fact that I worked first among people with whom I share a familial and cultural background.

Only years later have I done research in the kind of place far from home that is typical for anthropological fieldwork. When the anthropologists Linda and Jim Belote first introduced me to Saraguro in 2005, I was struck not by how different it was but by how familiar it felt. And by familiarity I don't mean "sameness"—the Saraguros' history and contemporary culture are not just a globalized mirror I hold up to see myself in some kind of narcissistic game of navel gazing. The familiarity is about the deep roots of human experience—love of life, care and compassion for other humans, striving for a good daily life. As with my own aunts, uncles, and cousins, Benigno, Ana Victoria, and the other Saraguros I visit see value in sharing stories and experiences. This love of stories is one of the threads connecting the people I write about in this book with the people of the Texas Hill Country I wrote about in my first book. The kind of anthropology I value shares this keen awareness: the data of anthropology have primarily been gleaned by anthropologists acting as engaged listeners in social worlds made up of the stories people tell about each other and about their places and their worlds.

In the last thirty years (and intermittently before that), anthropologists have engaged in a fair share of self-reflection about how we construct our ways of thinking about the world and how these constructions shape what we write. My training as an anthropologist began in the late 1980s after Clifford and Marcus (1986) edited the volume *Writing Culture: The Poetics and Politics of Ethnography*. This book, as well as many later volumes (see Marcus and Fischer 1986; Fox 1991; Behar and Gordon 1996; Behar 1997; and others) and ethnographies from around the same time (see Stoller and Olkes 1989; Brown 1991; Abu-Lughod 1993; Behar 1993; and others), challenged us to think about how we create our ideas and texts as anthropologists. The field of anthropology has increasingly, if sometimes nervously, shifted to allow space for reflection on the ethnographer's habits of research and writing as part of the discipline's world of thinking. For example, several edited volumes (McLean and Leibing 2007; Davis and Konner 2011; Waterston and Vesperi 2011) offer many thoughtful essays by practicing anthropologists that seek to expand the possible approaches to observing, thinking, and writing that make up the strands of an anthropological consciousness.

Instead of being an ethnography focused exclusively on the Saraguros, this book explores how contemporary globalization shapes my own life and thought as well as my Saraguro friends' responses to some basic question. Some of the questions we have explored together are

- What does it mean to live "the good life" in different cultural contexts?
- How do our work opportunities affect our pursuit of the good life?
- What is the value of the anthropological enterprise of translating the experiences of different cultures across cultural boundaries?
- How can anthropology's comparative approach be used to raise questions about the ways we tell stories and think and act in the world?
- Given that cultural anthropology is a discipline that uses one's own existence and perceptions as a basic tool for research, how does my life as an anthropologist, a U.S. citizen, a college professor, and a man from a background of poverty who now, along with his family, lives comfortably well in the northern United States shape how I understand the work I do in the field, in the classroom, and at the writing desk?

As I think about my travels between home and the physical and social worlds of Saraguro, several themes and metaphors engage my imagination. I introduced the idea of the technopelli in the prologue and will continue to explore this metaphor throughout the book. I am also drawn by the following themes and will explore them in what follows: work and the ways that it shapes our experience of time; stories, especially stories about place; the relationships between tradition and creativity; and the ways that anthropological consciousness gets made and employed in the contemporary world.

The pages that follow offer more details about the writer of these words than most ethnographic accounts conventionally do. I choose to be explicit about the ways that my being-in-the-world and my intellectual and emotional agenda set the conditions of my encounter with the Saraguro people because this feels the most truthful to my experiences as a traveler between different cultural settings. By highlighting my own engagements and practices in the process of ethnographic research and writing, I am foregrounding the strange position of the anthropologist as a liminal figure, someone who spends time and thinks between social worlds to create the odd combination of experience-near and experience-distant writing that is one hallmark of ethnography. Geertz highlights the challenge of this betweenness of ethnographic writing: "To grasp concepts that, for another people, are experience-near, and to do so well enough to place them in illuminating connection with experience-distant concepts theorists have fashioned to capture the general features of social life, is clearly a task at least as delicate, if a bit less magical, as putting yourself in someone else's skin" (1983, 58).

Paul Stoller points out that the best ethnographies position themselves and their author's experiences between worlds. He writes that when you have read a compelling work of ethnography, "you have immersed yourself in an ethnography that reaffirms the common threads of our humanity, which, in turn, deepens your sensitivities to the human condition. Considered in this light, ethnography can sometimes be a bridge that connects two worlds, binding two universes of meaning. It can be a path that entwines the distant lives of others to our more familiar being, a gift to the world" (2007, 181). Later, in his essay on the relationships among ethnography, memoir, imagination, and story, Stoller observes that "in ethnographies, memoirs, novels, and films anthropologists tell other people's stories. In so doing, as Adamu Jenitongo once reminded me, we also tell our own stories" (ibid., 188). The telling of our own stories, as anthropologists, inevitably derives both from the experience-near worlds of ethnographic fieldwork and the more distant agendas of thought that, while they may connect to the ideas and experiences of people we encounter in the field, also derive from our discipline and the academic world.

For now, I acknowledge that academics, journalists, and other popular writers have suggested that globalization kills place and that societies whose economies are caught up in large-scale processes inevitably lose their distinctive identities. However, many anthropologists, humanistic geographers, philosophers, and others have also argued that place making is an ongoing process following from human social activities in the landscape. My first book explored the concept of "emplacedness" in a rural region of the United States. When I talk to people in Saraguro, I also find a deep sense of commitment to the idea that places matter and contain interesting and important stories. Throughout this book, stories of place return as touchstones and guideposts for making sense of culture.

The people I visit in Saraguro actively think and talk about the relationships among tradition, creativity, change, and globalization. When Benigno and Ana Victoria point to something and say that it is either in keeping with the traditions of the community or varies in ways that might be seen as nontraditional, they perform an analysis of culture, creativity, and change just as an anthropologist does. The Saraguros, and indeed many indigenous societies of the Andes, are often popularly portrayed as "timeless" or "stuck in the past." My experience of Saraguro approaches to life, however, suggests dynamic, creative experimentation and reflection on how tradition does and does not serve contemporary needs. For example, when Ana Victoria creates a new necklace pattern or designs an entire matched ensemble of blouse, necklace, embroidered skirt, and earrings, she sees herself simultaneously as working within the vibrant handcraft traditions of her community and as a creative individual working within the opportunities and constraints of the contemporary world.

James Clifford's introduction to *Writing Culture* identifies "the historical predicament of ethnography, *the fact that it is always caught up in the invention, not the representation, of cultures*" (1986, 2, emphasis added). My intention in quoting Clifford is not to rehash critiques of representation but to point to the nature of an anthropological consciousness and the making of ethnographic writing as *invention* of culture. The Saraguro people I talk to and work with are inventors of a culture and an anthropological consciousness, as am I. We are all embedded in the process of re-weaving the world's meanings according to our experiences and understandings.

PLAN OF THIS BOOK

Chapter 2, "A Necklace, a Metaphor, and the Saraguro Context," introduces more fully the idea of *la vida matizada* (the blended life) and presents background information on the Saraguro people and region. You will find references to other works of anthropology that may be of interest for further exploration of academic voices on the Andean region.

Chapter 3, "*La Vida Matizada* and Work Life in a Globalizing Society," presents the experiences of three men. The first is Benigno Cango, a Saraguro man who has remained in his home community and who, with his accomplished artisan wife, Ana Victoria Sarango, has pieced together economic opportunities that permit him to live well while maintaining *la vida matizada*, a mode of life that he and other Saraguros state is their preferred way of living. The second, Maximo Sarango, Benigno's brother-in-law, has pursued a different economic path, one that has led him to spend much of each year living and working in the United States, first as a musician, and then later as a worker at an industrial dairy farm. His daily life is far from the desired state of *la vida matizada*. And I am the third, an anthropologist at the University of Minnesota Duluth who has had an uneven trajectory into the academic world, working first as a farm- and ranch hand, then as an environmental organizer, and eventually as a full-time college professor. This chapter presents each of us in our work and daily life contexts and meditates on the nature of work in the contemporary world.

Chapter 4, "Weaving *la Vida Matizada*: Beadwork and Cooperatives in Saraguro Women's Lives," shifts the focus to women's experience in Saraguro, especially by looking at the work of the members of an artisanal cooperative. Women in many of the small communities of Saraguro have formed cooperative organizations that provide social support and economic development for the women. The Saraguros practice several distinctive crafts, foremost being the creation of large, woven-bead necklaces called *collares* or *wallkas*. I spend my fieldwork seasons living and apprenticing with Ana Victoria Sarango, an accomplished artist who lives in the community of Tuncarta. This chapter combines Ana Victoria's life story with the story of Las Calcutas (named after Mother Teresa of Calcutta), one of several successful women's cooperatives in the Saraguro area.

Chapter 5, "Sweet Water and Exotic Fish: Ecological Imaginations in a World of Traveling Creatures," presents two legends told by a Saraguro storyteller, as well as the stories of invasive species in my home region of the Great Lakes of the United States.

Chapter 6, "On the Development and Value of an Anthropological Consciousness," opens with the story drawn from my field notes of an encounter in a Quito hostel with a traveling bunch of clown healers. The chapter also includes the story of a ceremony I attended in a cave said to be sacred to the Incas, located just outside the town of Saraguro. But it is a story once removed—told during an introductory anthropology class to highlight the difficulty of suspending judgment and maintaining a cultural relativist stance. The story also opens an opportunity for meditating on the creation of an anthropological consciousness as the goal of conducting anthropology and/or teaching and writing about cross-cultural experiences.

Following most of the substantive chapters of the book, I include what I call "interludes." The word "interlude," meaning "between play," suggests an approach that is different from the surrounding material. It also suggests a break from the main action of a play. With these pieces I offer an alternative ethnographic voice and eye. Each of these interludes seeks to push my descriptions out of the strictly narrative or analytic voice of the chapters to include images that expand and/or comment on the ideas of the book. Kokopelli, as a mythical figure, brings music and playfulness with him on his journeys; the technopelli, too, seeks to offer something in addition to straightforward analysis—these interludes move toward this objective.

The book concludes with an epilogue, a story told by my closest Saraguro friend, Benigno, that evokes many of the themes of the book and highlights the ongoing nature of our technopelli work together.

Interlude 1

THREE IMAGES OF TECHNOPELLI

In the early 20th century it was widely believed that "primitive" cultures would disappear. . . . However, at the beginning of the 21st century, tribal cultures, under whatever politically correct term is popular at the moment, are still with us and going strong. No longer primitive, many of these people are every bit as modern as the societies around them, but still have been able to maintain cultural, linguistic, and religious unity. The processes of globalization both threaten tribal societies and provide the means of their survival.

TED. C. LEWELLEN, *THE ANTHROPOLOGY OF GLOBALIZATION* (2002)

Calling upon the "shadow side" of fieldwork will likely shift the way ethnographic data is regarded. The data can no longer pretend to stand by themselves. . . . This reflects the illusory nature of an objective, unmediated relationship with reality. More profoundly, it destroys any pretensions of the transparency of description and language. It reminds us that the words we use and images we form are always "haunted" by other words, voices, and visions — by sensations, shapes, and colors that depend intimately on the particular personal, social, and cultural histories that make up who we are, often without our knowledge.

ELLEN CORIN, "PERSONAL TRAVELS THROUGH OTHERNESS," IN *THE SHADOW SIDE OF FIELDWORK* (MCLEAN AND LEIBING 2007)

*B*EFORE YOU READ WHAT I WANT TO SAY ABOUT the three photos here, I would like to invite you to take a moment to look at them and form your own ideas about what you see.

Benigno likes to fish. When I told him I do as well, we set out for an afternoon along the Río Hierba Buena. Benigno carried a small pack with two telescoping fishing poles, two small, empty plastic bags and a larger plastic bag (to be used, respectively, to hold bait and fish), some water, and fruit. I loaded my pack with a sweater (that I would not need as the day grew warm quickly), my Spanish dictionary, some water, and a bag with two oranges that Ana Victoria gave me.

"That will be all you eat for the afternoon," Ana Victoria said, laughing.

"Then I'll be really hungry tonight!" I said.

"I guess you better catch some fish!" she said.

We started along the Tio Loma road and turned onto a foot-path following above the general path of the river. We stopped at a circle of stones (*hera*) about six inches high surrounding a twelve-foot-wide area covered in flat cobblestones. Benigno said that this was a place for threshing grain. Years ago people laid the circle to keep the grain from getting dirty on the ground. They would lay the cut and dried stalks on the flat stones and stomp on them to shatter the grains. On a breezy day, they would then toss the threshed crop into the air so that the grains sifted down while the chaff blew away. There were a few fragments of old stalks, and Benigno showed me an empty head of a barley plant. Someone has continued to use the stone circle even to this day.

Benigno indicated where each community ended and the next began. Next to Tuncarta, on the same side of the river, is Tambopamba. Beyond Tambopamba is Oñacapac, separated only by a small stream that we crossed on a plank. Across the river from Oñacapac is Gurudel. Benigno pointed out these boundaries to orient me as a newcomer to the place. Each community, he said, has distinctive land resources as well as community personalities.

We stopped on the bridge over the river. I told Benigno the story of the Three Billy Goats Gruff. Because I did not know the

Spanish word for "troll," I called them "animals with sharp teeth and much hair that live under bridges and that eat people when they try to cross from one side to the other." The story delighted Benigno, and he asked for more details, including variants of the stories and information about who tells them and why.

"Immigrants to the United States from northern Europe carried the stories with them," I said. "Trolls are usually fierce and strong but stupid. There are many stories about people,

Benigno engrossed in an anthropological consciousness as he writes down cuentos *(tales) of trolls, just as I will become engrossed after supper when he tells me* leyendas *(legends) about places in the mountains.*

especially smart young girls, who escape from them by being clever."

"Una nota!" he said, the phrase he and Ana Victoria had been using to tease me every time I stopped to write something in my pocket notebook. He wanted to write down the troll stories. I gave him an extra notepad I had in my pack.

"Now I am an anthropologist, too!" he said.

This exchange reminded me that, while I conceive of myself as a participant and observer when I do fieldwork, I am also the observed. Saraguros, like any people with whom anthropologists work, are as curious about the people who visit as the visitors are about them.

A few evenings later, Ana Victoria, Benigno, and I sat at the kitchen table after finishing supper. We had been joking

Ana Victoria engaging with the technology I bring to the field, enacting her own technopelli persona in the between space we create together.

about all the technology I carry when I visit. I gave Ana Victoria the tiny computer I had brought with me to use for making field notes. Ana Victoria played with this technology while wearing my sunglasses, bent in concentration a moment after she had coined for me the nickname "el hombre de muchas cosas" ("the man of many things"). In that moment she was fully captivated by one of the many things I bring with me, her focus similar to photos I have seen of myself engrossed in beading.

At these moments, Benigno, Ana Victoria, and I had no sense of the distinction between observer and observed. We spent much of the time during that fishing outing and evening at the kitchen table trading those roles back and forth fluidly as I asked about what we were seeing, as Benigno asked me to describe how I go fishing in my home community, and as Ana Victoria quizzed me about the ways I used these technologies at home. At any given moment, one of us would play the role of recorder and the other the role of storyteller. This back-and-forth fluid dynamic represents one of the truest expressions of the work I do as a traveler and anthropologist, and it is out of this that my sense of friendship with Benigno and Ana Victoria has been planted and grown.

In these photos neither Benigno nor Ana Victoria looks at the camera. They are fully taken up with a post-joke moment

Shadows are one way to represent the technopelli—a persona created in the ethnographic encounters that happen when cultural spaces and identities overlap with one another.

of engaging with the specific material, ideas, and intellectual curiosities that my presence in their lives has brought to the table. They are as engaged in drawing out stories, ideas, and meanings as any traveling anthropologist. The technopelli role is neither singular nor exclusive to anthropologists. As the two epigraphs at the beginning of this interlude suggest, the people anthropologists work with have their own experiences, interests, and expressions regarding life in the contemporary world, and any work of ethnography that does not make space for these feels incomplete.

The technopelli is a shadow or silhouette because it is not a person but a persona—a mask that anthropologists and the people we work with in the contemporary world put on and take off as needed. In the end, our lives move on, but the image of the technopelli lingers in the ways that each of us—Benigno, Ana Victoria, and David—make use of the stories and insights we generate together to make our own versions of *la vida matizada*, the blended life.

CHAPTER TWO

A Necklace, a Metaphor, and the Saraguro Context

matiz m (pl -tices) shade, hue, nuance
matizar tr (diversos colores) to blend; (un color, un sonido)
shade; (en cuanto al color) match

BANTAM NEW COLLEGE REVISED SPANISH
AND ENGLISH DICTIONARY

*If we don't start to think and reflect as our elders used to do, and who
used to say "lift your foot up and look at the earth you're standing on,"
we won't get very far. We need to do this.*

LUIS MACAS, "THE ECUADORIAN INDIGENOUS MOVEMENT"
(2000)

T HE *WALLKA*, OR *COLLAR*, OR NECKLACE, SITS ON THE
table. A large circle of beads that took me three weeks to
make, the *wallka* shades from black, through hues of dark green to candy
apple green, then from white through shades of pink to dark plum purple,
then to black and dark blue through cerulean, back to white again, and
from matte yellow through brick red, terminating once again in black. The
overall effect resembles lightning bolts of oddly colored rainbows. It was
slow going, but now I have a complete example of each of the four-color
patterns that my teacher, Ana Victoria, calls *matizado*, blended or matched.
The entire time I worked, I meditated on what she means by *matizado* and
at the same time watched as people went about their daily work in Tuncarta, an indigenous, agricultural community in southern Ecuador. As the

necklace came close to being finished, it dawned on me that I was weaving a metaphor to help make sense of the numerous comings and goings I see every day, a metaphor for the preferred way of life for my friends here. "The blended life," a life that shades satisfactorily from one activity to another, appears to be a useful model for "the good life."

The idea of this metaphor came the morning after Ana Victoria and Benigno took me to the graduation party of a cousin. After dark we walked down the valley to a house illuminated by strings of lights. Loudspeakers and a stage filled one side of the yard. The family had hired the musical group of Benigno's brothers and their friends to play for the party. After we arrived and ate, Benigno sat on the ground next to a young man whose hair was cut short, a likely sign that he had been traveling or working outside the community of Tuncarta, a fact confirmed after Benigno shook hands and began talking to him. Benigno asked how the man had liked being in the United States, to which he gave a noncommittal grunt. They talked about the work he had done on a dairy farm. He described long shifts moving cattle into the milking parlor, cleaning the udders and attaching the milking machines, monitoring the machines as they stripped the milk, removing the "claws" of the machines, sending the cows on, and processing another batch of two dozen, all of this for eight to ten hours at a time. Benigno expressed surprise and distaste.

"How could you do this same thing over and over, every day, all day long?" Benigno asked.

That question opened an insight into the pace and rhythms of work I had been immersed in as I watched people come and go. Benigno has chosen to remain in his home community, while a second family member, Maximo, brother-in-law to Benigno, travels regularly between Ecuador and the United States to work at an industrial-scale dairy farm in the Midwest. I work as a college professor and anthropological researcher. Benigno, Maximo, and I are each choosing to live and work in specific ways shaped by opportunities and our values. Benigno's approach to work life does not necessarily maximize his economic opportunities, but it also does not require ways of living that seem to be alien and disruptive of living the good life as imagined locally. Maximo's approach increases the potential for economic gain but has many undesired effects that challenge ideas of a good life and that result in frictions, stresses, and challenges that force Maximo to redefine his aspirations. The work rhythms required for my job are certainly part of the same globalized system as Benigno's and Maximo's; however, I receive the benefits of economic opportunity, while still retaining some power over my daily life. My own work life opportunities and choices position me within the "winning" end of a globalized system, wherein I largely control the scheduling and pace of my work time while still earning a large enough income to be part of the comfortable global middle class. However, like Maximo, I must travel, sometimes for extended periods, away from my family to conduct the research that is an essential part of my work life.

Doing fieldwork and developing friendships with people who do incredible things in relation to artisanal work, farming, subsistence, and community making reinvigorates my mental and emotional energy. I have aspired for years to do more in the way of raising food and living in what might be seen as *la vida matizada*, a closer harmony with my local landscape and community. Seeing what Benigno and his brothers, sisters, mother, and wife accomplish on a daily basis in terms of raising their own food and cultivating community with their neighbors inspires me.

As a traveler between these different work worlds and daily lives, I have arrived at that place that a comparative, anthropological perspective often comes to—seeing ideas and behaviors that can be identified in metaphors that resonate for understanding culture, even when people living within any given cultural context would not necessarily articulate the idea in precisely those ways. *La vida matizada*—the good life as a blend of diverse work opportunities, social embeddedness, and a satisfying sense of a person's ability to shape how he or she lives—has emerged as a viable metaphor for understanding what I have learned in Saraguro. While my Saraguro friends do not articulate the idea of *la vida matizada* directly, they do embrace my descriptions of it as resonant with their ideas and aspirations for the lives they seek to create for themselves.

THE SARAGURO CONTEXT

Saraguro is a canton of Loja Province, located in southern Ecuador (see maps 2.1 and 2.2). About thirty thousand people live there, including indigenous people who consider themselves descendents of the Incas and who call themselves Saraguros and mixed-heritage descendants of Spanish immigrants identified as *mestizos*, "mixed," or *blancos*, "whites," by the indigenous people (Belote and Belote 1999; Macas, Belote, and Belote 2003). Linda Belote (1978) presents the earliest and most complete discussion of indigenous-white relations. In the 1960s and 1970s Belote found that the Saraguros, through land ownership and a fair amount of cultural autonomy in comparison to other indigenous groups in the high-

Labels in the image:
BUENOS AIRES
SANTIAGO
Oceano Pacífico
SÃO PAULO
LA PAZ
LIMA
SARAGURO
QUITO
00° 00' 00"
MEXICO
MIAMI
Oceano Atlántico
NEW YORK
SAN FRANCISCO
ST. JOHNS
DULUTH
VANCOUVER
South-side-up map of the Americas
J. Belote 2012

MAP 2.1. *Location of Saraguro in the Western Hemisphere.*
Map by James Belote.

lands, were not as poverty stricken or suppressed as other native communities. The indigenous population lives primarily, though not exclusively, in the rural areas of the canton, while the nonindigenous population lives primarily, though not exclusively, in the city of Saraguro. The city serves as the center of commercial activities for both the indigenous and nonindigenous people. Indigenous Saraguros also have population concentrations in Zamora-Chinchipe Province, located in the Amazon watershed to the east of Saraguro proper. Several thousand indigenous Saraguros live abroad.

Indigenous Saraguros live by a combination of farming, artisanal work (especially spinning and weaving, beadwork, and making skirts and embroidered blouses), local day labor, and—increasingly over the last twenty-five years—remittances from abroad. Anywhere from 10 to 25 percent (Cueva 2005) of the adult population live and work in the United States, Spain, Brazil, and other foreign countries. A small but growing number of Saraguros have sought advanced education, locally, within Ecuador, and abroad. In addition to producing nearly two hundred teachers, Saraguros have become doctors, dentists, veterinarians, lawyers, and agronomists and have taken up other professions. This newer arena for work creates dynamics for identity formation that include alternative relations to work rhythms and daily life and require different strategies for maintaining ethnic identity, such as blending careers with the cultural practices of agriculture, community service, and collective labor (*minga*) among extended family networks. An active cultural revitalization movement indicates an increasing desire among Saraguros to think about and consciously enact the components of their culture they find crucial to preserve in the face of modernization and change.

MAP 2.2. *Location of Saraguro in Ecuador. Map by James Belote.*

Saraguros strongly identify themselves as an indigenous ethnic group. The genesis of this distinctive ethnic identity is a complex result of historical processes extending to Inca and Spanish colonization of the Andean region. The claim of Incan heritage by the indigenous people of the area is complicated, as the evidence suggests that the ethnic identity of Saraguros grew from a mixture of Incan *mitamaes* (relocated workers) and several indigenous groups who lived in the area before and during the Incan period (see Belote 1984, 1–5, 52–65; and Ogburn 2008). Saraguro identity is expressed in counterpoint to a white-*mestizo* (*blanco*) identity (Belote 1978), a practice consistent with much of the ethnographic evidence on Andean peoples (see, e.g., the contrast between indigenous Runakuna and Misti [*mestizo*] in Allen 2002, 12–15; also see Belote and Belote 1984a for an extensive discussion of the fluid performance of Saraguro ethnicity).

In addition to self-identifying through language, plus family and community connections and obligations, people express ethnicity visibly and self-reflectively in Saraguro dress and hairstyle. Saraguro women signal ethnicity by wearing black, pleated skirts and embroidered blouses. Men demonstrate ethnicity with dark, short pants. For daily wear both men and women tend to wear black, small-brimmed hats. Older Saraguros, and others for special occasions, wear a large, sombrero-style felt hat painted white with black patterns on the underside of the brim. For example, when I helped the women of one artist's cooperative prepare to apply to attend an international folk market, they wanted their photographs taken with these hats. They said they wanted to present themselves as "proper" indigenous women.

Saraguro men and women both wear a single long braid (*jimba*) down the center of their backs. Because Saraguros consider the braid such an important marker of ethnicity, Benigno was able to identify the man with the haircut (described at the beginning of this chapter) as a Saraguro who had traveled abroad, where Saraguros sometimes cut their hair to reduce social friction (for a discussion of the *jimba* as a metaphor for Saraguro identity, see Macas, Belote, and Belote 2003).

Many Saraguros identify practices common in the 1950s and 1960s as traditional. The definition of "traditional" is a life based on low-technology agriculture raising corn, beans, potatoes, and other, minor crops as well as herding dairy cattle and sheep. Values commonly seen as traditional include emphasis on collective effort, solidarity, reciprocity, family, hard work, harmony, and respect for nature (Vacacela 2002; Macas, Belote, and Belote 2003, 223–228; Belote and Belote 2005; for a description of historical arrangements for labor among Saraguros, as well as a discussion of adaptations of work patterns related to colonizing efforts in the rain forest east of Saraguro, see esp. Belote 1984, chaps. 5–10).

The selection of the 1950s and 1960s as the time of tradition likely grows out of the extensive social changes that came in the 1970s–1990s as all of Ecuador experienced agricultural modernization and economic booms and busts associated with the discovery of oil in Ecuador's portion of the Amazon basin. The subsequent development of an oil-based energy sector brought electricity to the Saraguro region and led to enhanced roads and transportation infrastructure, drawing Saraguros more fully into the national culture and discussions about indigenous ethnicity and national identity. As is the case throughout Latin America (see, e.g., Gordillo and Hirsch 2003; Yashar 2005; Viatori 2007), indigenous people increasingly define identity in conversation with national and international forces, making the seemingly isolated Saraguro lifeways of the 1950s and 1960s appear static and nostalgically traditional.

From at least the 1970s onward, a growing indigenous rights movement throughout Latin America has reshaped indigenous expressions of self and ethnicity. In fact, in her chapter on Ecuador, Yashar (2005) calls the work of indigenous activists in the country "Latin America's Strongest Indigenous Movement." She describes the strands that fed into the 1990 formation of a Confederation of Indigenous Nationalities of Ecuador (CONAIE). The confederation formed with the highly visible participation of Dr. Luis Alberto Macas Ambuldi, a Saraguro activist/organizer. Macas was elected in 1996 to the Ecuadorian Congress and was later appointed agricultural minister.

With many other active Saraguro citizens, contemporary Saraguro ethnicity has become politically deployed, complicated, and engaged in regional and national conversations about power in democratic nation-states. As in any society, there are a variety of political viewpoints, parties, and organizations in Saraguro and Ecuador. Federación Interprovincial de Indígenas Saraguros (FIIS), Pachakutik–Nuevo País, and others serve as organizing points for the political activities. Politics, indigenous and otherwise, are lively in the community of Saraguro. Ana Victoria and Benigno often head off in the afternoons and evenings to community and political meetings, both within their small village of Tuncarta and in the city center of the canton.

With the exception of one meeting early in my fieldwork, before I knew enough to follow what was happening, I have not been invited along. Though Benigno and Ana Victoria trust my motives, many of the community members do not know me well, and there is enough history of meddlesome outsiders intervening in indigenous political lives that I have not pressed for invitations to such meetings.

The Saraguros themselves tell and will tell the story of their political challenges and aspirations. For example, Macas discusses his remarkable political career, both in his own writings and with the anthropologists Linda and Jim Belote (see Macas 1991; Macas, Belote, and Belote 2003). In an article available on the web in both Spanish and English, he outlines the rise of indigenous activism in Ecuador (Macas 2000). He ties such activism explicitly to the need to honor traditions of the past while asserting dynamic possibilities of creative engagement with the present and future. In essence, he argues for an anthropological perspective that culture is a dynamic, ongoing, performative invention rather than simply a static acceptance of inherited ideas and practices:

> Despite all the talk of "*Shuk shungulla, shuk maquilla, shuk yuyailla*" ("one heart, one hand, one thought," in Kichwa), they are values that don't exist, that aren't taught in school, college or university. Values are an integral part of our identity.
>
> This crisis in values is the cause of the global crisis as it stops us acting on the basis of who we are and what we think and instead of what others have made us think we are, which in this era makes us easy prey. We don't know whether it's an era of change or a change of eras, but it's a time of conflict—we are clear about that and so we act accordingly. If, say, in ten years' time indigenous people haven't stopped to think and reflect about ourselves we're going to disappear in a stream of homogeneity. That's what we call the crisis of transition. Either we identify ourselves as who we are and decide to really be what our elders have bequeathed us (the dream of being an original nation in our own right, and so on, while gathering and benefiting from the wealth of universal knowledge available to all) or we disappear as individuals and as nations. (Macas 2000)

The work of Macas and other indigenous political leaders in Ecuador—and, indeed, throughout Latin America—offers clear evidence that the political fate of their peoples is contested and that they can create engaged and productive debate and resistance in the forum of nation-states, corporations, and transnational political and economic agendas. Even when individuals do not participate directly in political or social movement activities, the question of what it means to be a contemporary indigenous citizen of a nation-state is present in many Saraguro peoples' minds. If the nearly nightly conversations about world politics that I have had with Benigno and his extended family are any indication, the Saraguros are savvy and informed and engaged with the political arrangements that shape their lives.

Saraguros have been affected by national and international development projects that have reshaped the contours of Ecuadorian life. The national economy has long depended on export-focused agriculture but has shifted in the last few decades with the discovery of oil in the Ecuadorian Amazon. Striffler's (2002) work on the history of United Fruit Company's development in Ecuador explores the impact of agricultural modernization in Ecuador. Sawyer (2004) describes the transformations wrought by the oil industry on Ecuador's economy and national identity. Whitten (1985) provides an earlier analysis of the effects on indigenous peoples of development in the Amazon, especially in the northern and central parts of the basin. Several documentaries, especially *Trinkets and Beads* (Walker 1996), as well as *Crude: The Real Cost of Oil* (Belinger 2009), convey the impacts of oil development on the indigenous people of the Ecuadorian Amazon. Although oil drilling has focused on the Amazon, it has affected the entire country, as up to 50 percent of the funds to run the Ecuadorian government come from oil revenues.

While these works focus on economic activities based in the lowland areas of Ecuador, the effects of these developments reverberate through the country as national policy continues to favor transnational corporations and the national government. Numerous authors explore indigenous relationships to the Ecuadorian state, resistance, and social action. Useful resources on these topics include works by Macas (1991, 2000) and Zamosc (1994), writings by Korovkin (1997a, 1997b, 2001) and Yashar (2005), a volume edited by Clark and Becker (2007), and others. Korovkin, especially, explores how indigenous cultural forms such as communal decision making and diversified economic practices continue into the present and help to shape community and ethnic identities.

FRICTIONS OF MIGRATION AND GLOBALIZATION

Migration within Ecuador has been part of Saraguro subsistence strategies for many decades. In the 1990s migration for work expanded internationally—slowly, at first, to the United States and more quickly to Spain. A growing literature (Kyle 2000; Meisch 2002; Bacacela 2003; Miles 2004; Belote and Belote 2005; Herrera, Carrillo, and Torres 2005) focuses on this transnational migration from Ecuador, though only Bacacela and the Belotes focus directly on the Saraguros. A United Nations–sponsored study (Solimano 2003) identified Ecuador as one of the top twenty developing nations in terms of total dollars sent home by migrants working in other countries. According to a U.S. Congressional Budget Office report (2005), remittances to Ecuador were $1.4 billion in 2002. This accounted for 6 percent of the country's entire gross domestic product. The remittances were 12 percent more than direct foreign investment and were six times more than the amount of foreign aid the country received. The U.S. portion represents the largest share (nearly 47 percent) of remitted monies, with Spain accounting for most of the rest (about 41 percent; see the Center for Latin American Monetary Studies 2010). Transnational migration clearly has significant financial effects on Ecuadorians, including the Saraguro people (World Bank 2011).

Migration also raises significant questions about how to live the good life as community members encounter various models of daily life and labor practices in countries as varied as the United States, Spain, Brazil, and others. Anna Tsing (1993, 2005) examines these kinds of global connections and develops the metaphor of "friction," which occurs when individuals and institutions with culturally specific histories encounter the universalizing aspirations of global connections, practices, and ideas:

> Capitalism, science, and politics all depend on global connections. Each spreads through aspirations to fulfill *universal* dreams and schemes. Yet this is a particular kind of universality: It can only be charged and enacted in the sticky materiality of practical encounters. . . . The specificity of global connections is an ever-present reminder that universal claims do not actually make everything everywhere the same. Global connections give *grip* to universal aspirations. . . . At this confluence, universals and particulars come together to create the forms of capitalism with which we live. (Tsing 2005, 1, 4; emphases in original)

Tsing suggests that important ethnographic and critical insights emerge through exploring the contradictions that arise when people experience contemporary globalization. Friction as the micro-level contact point between the direct and real experiences of people on the ground with macro-level forces becomes a productive space both for storytelling and for the active listening characteristic of the form of ethnography that I am here calling a "technopelli" approach. My role as a traveler in the community highlights many of the kinds of frictions Tsing explores.

My presence offers part of the grit my Saraguro acquaintances and friends use to think about their lives and the dynamics of globalization.

They point this out frequently. For example, when I arrived in Saraguro for a visit in 2009, I looked for a bus to Tuncarta (located a few miles outside the town center), and soon one pulled up next to Mama Cuchara's (a local restaurant cooperative). The driver, Miguel, said the bus would leave at 3:30 for the trip out to Tuncarta, Oñacapac, and Ñamarin. He asked if I preferred to hire a car to drive me, and said it would cost $4.

"How much for the bus?" I asked.

"Thirty cents," he said, so I bought a soda and sat in the square to watch people until it was time for the bus to go.

Miguel came back to the bus around 3:30. Only one woman, who had a long piece of gray PVC pipe to haul with her, had joined me to wait for the bus.

"Only you two?" Miguel said incredulously.

"I don't know," I said and shrugged. We waited a while, in hopes of more paying passengers.

"What's in the suitcase?" he asked, eyeing the rather large and very heavy bag.

"My clothes," I said. "And gifts for my friends." We had already established that I had been to Tuncarta before.

He paused a moment, then said, "Well, maybe if we get to know each other, then next time you come back I'll be one of your friends to bring gifts to!" and he chuckled.

"Perhaps," I said and laughed, too.

A moment of joking underscores the remnants of colonialism implicit in the kind of work anthropologists do. I am acutely aware that I am an outsider arriving with a few gifts. I hope that the people of this community will accept or at least tolerate my presence. I don't mean to overplay the idea of me as a colonial influence—the folks of this community have many ways that they access ideas and goods and attitudes from U.S. and global cultures. Saraguro is full of imported trucks, plastic dinner plates, U.S. films and television, and more. These all have a much greater impact than I do with my few gifts, questions, and the small ways I contribute to the local economy by carrying beadwork to the United States to sell and by paying for my room and board.

But I am also enmeshed and empowered by the global realities that make it easy for me to travel to this place whenever I want while people from Saraguro can travel to my country legally only under rare circumstances. Maximo's situation, for example, where he has secured a permanent worker's visa, is uncommon. When the women's cooperative selected Ana Victoria to attend the Santa Fe International Folk Market in 2010 to represent their work, Ana Victoria received a formal letter of invitation from the market. Even with this letter, Ana Victoria had to go through a complicated process of proving she was married, owned land, and had sufficient funds in her bank account to indicate that she was not desperate for work in the United States. She twice visited the embassy in Guayaquil (an hours-long bus ride to the coast). She received a travel visa only after Linda Belote and officials at the Santa Fe Market secured a letter of support for the application from a U.S. senator.

In the next chapter I explore these complex frictions shaping people's encounters with the realities of a globalized system that encourages the flow of goods and capital but restricts the flow of humans.

Las Mujeres de Teresa de Calcuta of Tuncarta display some of their necklaces as they prepare to send them to the Santa Fe International Folk Art Market in 2010. The cooperative plans to build a women's cultural center with future earnings.

Petrona, Benigno's mother, on her way to town, wearing the de colores *pattern, universally considered the "most traditional" by the women, along with strands of metallic, gold-finished beads.*

Ana Victoria modeling a variation of an elegante *(elegant) necklace she had just designed.* Elegantes *are usually made to be sold rather than worn by Saraguro women themselves.*

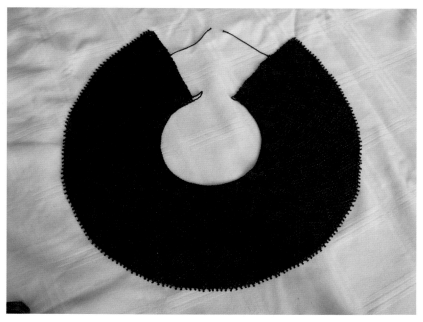

This model was in widespread production beginning about 2008. The website www.saraguro.org/beadwork.htm, created and maintained by Linda and Jim Belote, offers numerous examples of styles from the 1960s to the present.

Laughter, joking, and high spirits often fill the meetings of the cooperative.

Aleja Medina González, with her daughter Paulina, invented this pattern, called fresas *(strawberries), after studying photos in an art book Linda Belote brought to the women.*

Rosa Medina Sarango beading on the patio of her home. When the members of the cooperative are unable to attend meetings, they work on their own time on pieces for the group.

Mariana Lozano in 2009 working on a necklace commissioned by a nonbeading Saraguro woman who lives in the Amazon.

Mariana Lozano in the 1980s; this photo was taken by a visiting anthropologist. Courtesy of Mariana Lozano.

In 2009 Mariana allowed me to copy this photo of her family from the 1970s. It shows Mariana and her siblings with her mother and father nearly forty years ago. Courtesy of Mariana Lozano.

Ana Victoria considers how best to display her cooperative's beadwork as she sets up for the 2010 Santa Fe International Folk Art Market.

The anthropologist Linda Belote and Ana Victoria Sarango review the inventory list at the 2010 Santa Fe International Folk Art Market.

Ana Victoria visits with an artist/vendor from China at the 2010 Santa Fe Market.

Luz Magdalena Macas Minga wearing the cara-coles pattern necklace she made for herself.

Ana Victoria with Benigno's sister, Nila, and my daughter, Selene, at the beading table. It is not unusual for one or more people who are learning beading techniques to join Ana Victoria each day at the table on the porch to work.

All the artists at the Santa Fe Market identify a selected piece that they feel represents their best work. This piece, chosen by Ana Victoria, is labeled "Artist's Choice" and displayed prominently for sale.

CHAPTER THREE

La Vida Matizada *and Work*
Life in a Globalizing Society

*The rhythm that is proper to capital is the rhythm of producing
(everything: things, men, people, etc.) and destroying (through wars,
through* progress, *through inventions and brutal interventions, through
speculation, etc.). It is often said: "Yes, it was like this or that in the old
days; then the world changed. . . ." This isn't wrong, but it does not go
beneath the surface; in fact there were, as we have seen, great rhythms
of historical time: apology for the body and following that negation
of the body — exaltation of love and pleasure then depreciation and
apology for frivolity — taste for and then refusal of violence, etc.
Capital replaced these alternatives with the conflicting dualities of
production and destruction, with increasing priority for the destructive capacity that comes at its peak and is raised to a world scale.*

HENRI LEFEBVRE, "THE MANIPULATIONS OF TIME,"

IN *RHYTHMANALYSIS* (2004)

*We must start by acknowledging that work swims in culture and
alters in response to a history far broader than that of work alone.
By culture we mean shared understandings and the representations
in symbols and objects. Culture permeates work in beliefs concerning
which organizations of work are feasible, effective, and/or desirable;
classifications of work as good or bad; grading of work's products;
expectations of proper behavior of bosses and subordinates; standards
of proper rewards for effort; and much more.*

CHRIS TILLY AND CHARLES TILLY,

WORK UNDER CAPITALISM (1998)

*T*HE FIRST TIME I STAYED WITH BENIGNO AND ANA Victoria, in December 2005, we walked to Hierba Buena to see Benigno's farmland. Along the way we talked about the work he does and looked at plants. He provided so much information that I could not keep track of it all without taking frequent notes in the little spiral notebook I always keep in one of my technopelli pockets.

Hierba Buena is the name of the river and also the name of the area around the river. We walked along the Tio Loma road for a while and then turned onto a footpath to the river. As we descended, we passed an old man sitting next to a plunging creek and playing a big drum.

"Why are you playing here?" Benigno asked.

"To entertain the others who are coming up the hill," he said.

We continued on and passed three women and two men climbing.

"They are musicians who will be playing at the festival in a few days," Benigno said.

Benigno pointed out a distant cleft in the river valley where a high waterfall crashes into a plunge pool that forms a lovely grotto. He said the place got its name, La Virgen Kaka, from an apparition that appeared about three hundred years ago. He told the story:

> Many years ago, a statue of the Virgin was dropped as it was being carried across the river. Nobody knew how to swim well enough to retrieve the statue. One day a soldier, a black man from the coast where swimming is more common, was traveling through the area. The people offered to pay him to retrieve the statue. He dove into the pool below the falls. Then he saw the figure of a woman in the rock at the far side of the water. She was beautiful and graceful and emanated a light that drew him forward. He saw that it was Mary, the mother of Jesus. As he approached to touch her hand, she withdrew into the stone. He, too, entered the rock, and they are both still there, their shapes outlined in the flowing forms of blackened stones in the cliff behind the pool.

Devoted visitors still make offerings of flower arrangements (*ramos*) and candles in a small chapel near the falls. A festival takes place there every year.

As we walked on, we passed by a place where someone had been working with a chainsaw. He had cut about thirty ten-foot-long boards from eucalyptus logs and stacked them to dry, with a bark-covered piece on top to shed water. The boards were amazingly uniform considering the worker had used a chainsaw for milling them. Later we saw a similar stack that Benigno had made and was letting dry so he could rebuild the little house where he keeps his chickens.

"Do you want to see my bees?" Benigno asked as we passed the entrance of a small ravine.

We walked fifty yards to a spot where bees had made a hive under the roots of a tree. A stick pointed prominently out of the hole, I thought as part of the honey extracting process.

"No," Benigno said. "I put that there to warn people to beware and not to disturb the hive."

We climbed the hillside, and Benigno pointed out a jicama (*Pachyrhizus erosus*, a vining plant whose tuberous roots are edible). Further up the hill we saw a tree he called a *luma* (*Pouteria caimito*, a tree species found throughout the Andes.) Benigno said its fruit is a prized treat in Saraguro, but the fruit was months from being ready.

From above us, squash plants cascaded down the hillside. Benigno said he interplanted these with corn, which I saw later, as well as with peas and fava beans. We found one ripe squash, a big green and white mottled one. We picked it to take back to make for lunch the next day.

"Do you eat the seeds of the squash, too?" I asked.

"Yes," he said. "A typical food of the Saraguros is potatoes served with a sauce made of ground squash seeds."

After we had traveled about thirty minutes from the house, we climbed to a clearing where his chickens stay. Three walls of the remains of a tiny two-story house tucked against the side of the hill, with a recently made structure of eucalyptus poles inside it. A piece of plastic stretched across to make a roof. Inside, a niche carved into the hill served as storage place for a sack of dried corn. Benigno fed the chickens and pointed out the poles he lashed together for the birds to climb to roost in a nearby tree. He grabbed an empty bag stashed into the wall to carry the squash.

Until he died twenty years ago, Benigno's grandfather lived in this house, which seems fairly remote from Tuncarta but lies in a peaceful spot, with only the sounds of the frogs in the trees and the running river below. We descended to the stream where Benigno's horse, cow, and calf grazed. He pulled a stake from the ground and led the calf to drink; then he did the same for the cow. The horse was picketed close enough to access the water whenever he wanted some.

"We come to give them water twice a day," Benigno said.

The farm contains Benigno's main fields for corn. He and Ana Victoria grow enough corn that they rarely need to buy it. That is an amazing feat, considering that they eat *mote* (boiled hominy) at almost every meal. Benigno's interplanting of corn with squash and legumes is the Three Sisters approach to cultivation common to many Native American societies in North America. The farm has three fields, perhaps 50 × 125 feet each. They don't usually need to purchase corn, carrots, cabbage, or lettuce. On the other side of the river sits a small house that belongs to Benigno's mother, though she now lives in Tuncarta. The building houses only stones used for grinding corn and wheat.

As we started back I told Benigno that I thought they had a really good life, and he thanked me. He said he hoped to build a house in Hierba Buena, with gardens, a *cancha* (playing field), and perhaps a small restaurant for tourists to eat at, but he said that he doesn't have the money to carry out his plans. He does construction work and other jobs around Tuncarta, and Ana Victoria does craft work, but he thinks he needs to finish a university education to do better. He took classes for a year long ago but pointed out that he lacks money to pay for more education for himself, especially now that his children are reaching university age.

WORK LIFE, DAILY LIFE, AND RHYTHMANALYSIS

With this introduction to Benigno's arrangements for raising much of his food, I began to meditate on how work and daily life interweave in Saraguro. Later, as I got to know Benigno's brother-in-law, Maximo, and learned about how he makes his living on a large-scale dairy farm in the United States, I decided to write about how culture and contemporary global realities shape ideas regarding time, work rhythms, and everyday life. The idea of "rhythmanalysis," conceived by the French thinker Henri Lefebvre (2004), provides a sounding board for making sense of these disparate experiences of time, work, and everyday life. An article by Linda Belote and Jim Belote (1984b) offers some context regarding how Saraguros in the past have preferred to organize their work lives. It is also useful to have some context for Maximo's work in U.S. industrial agriculture and my own work as a university professor.

After laying out these contexts, I describe Benigno's daily work rhythms and Maximo's experiences as he has travels regularly between Ecuador and the United States to work on an industrial-scale dairy farm. In Saraguro land is traditionally inherited bilaterally, with both male and female children inheriting wealth from parents. This fact becomes important in the contrast between Benigno's and Maximo's work options. Benigno, as the only heir on the side of his father's family (his own father died young—with Benigno the only child; I tell this story in chap. 5), inherited enough land to make himself nearly self-sufficient in terms of foods such as potatoes, cabbage, cheese, and beans. Maximo's smaller family inheritance (which Ana Victoria describes in chap. 4), was divided between him; his sister, Ana Victoria; and another brother. Maximo's land resources have been less substantial, and he has consequently pursued strategies more tied to transnational work opportunities. He also parlayed an earlier cultural trip to the United States to play music into a longer-term legal work visa. I describe my own work rhythms here as I pull together three disparate work experiences in the story of building a house in Saraguro. The house serves as a friction-filled site, following Tsing's (2005) metaphor, where three time senses and strategies for living intersect.

Until my appointment in 2006 to a tenure-track position in academia, I spent my work life wandering from one work opportunity to another, working as hired farm-/ranch hand in Texas, picking apples at an orchard in Wisconsin, working as hired labor on a Wisconsin dairy farm, marketing farm vegetables, doing editorial work, and teaching part-time. The fact that I have spent a number of years as a migrant laborer is a major reason for my interest in exploring this topic in the lives of my Saraguro acquaintances.

I am also compelled to think about these things because of my own family background. My father's father, as the youngest of nine children, did not inherit any of the land the family had homesteaded in the Texas Hill Country. He struggled with poverty his entire life, and many of his thirteen children, including my father, also struggled with poverty—a fact that haunts me into the present and makes my work life as a professor something that I reflect on frequently. Why have I been able to construct a viable economic life out of the work of anthropological research, writing, and teaching when so many of my own family members have struggled? What is my contribution to the world as an academic who has constructed his vision of a good life based on intellectual labor? How does the work life of an anthropologist differ from the people we often work with and write about?

The uneven experience of globalized work patterns struck home as I worked on early drafts of this book during a week when my house was receiving a new roof after sustaining hail damage. Because I had insurance on the home, I received nearly $7,000 from the insurance company to replace the roof, an amount that at the time of the repairs (2007) was roughly equivalent to the annual per capita gross domestic product of Ecuador (U.S. Central Intelligence Agency 2010). I hired a company to replace the roof, and when the workers showed up to do the job, they turned out to be Latino migrant laborers. In talking to one of the workers, I learned that he was Honduran, very likely in the United States without papers. He did not tell me this directly, but his avoidance of certain topics strongly suggested this. These workers spent two days in the hot sun working on my roof while I spent two days working on an early version of this chapter, largely at my kitchen table, surrounded by the regular rhythms of my family's everyday life. The men on my roof had no recourse to an experience of work as incorporated into daily life. They traveled from state to state and rarely stayed in one place long enough to have a life outside the rhythms of work. The men did not even know where they were. They asked me the name of the large lake (Lake Superior) they could see from the roofs of the houses they worked on. The workers had no orientation points for a sense of place in the place that I called home. One implication of globalization of work is that in the United States we rely on these kinds of negations of daily life among certain groups of people to maintain our own positions of privilege. Although I did not know in advance that the roofing company I hired would use migrant workers, I became complicit, like most U.S. citizens, in dehumanizing daily life for transitory workers.

For Benigno, Maximo, and me, our work lives are tied up in networks of capital that weave together the products of our labor (milk for the commercial food system, ecotourist destinations, scholarly representations of culture, college-educated U.S. citizens who travel to Ecuador for field school training, mission service trips, or Peace Corps service). In addition to drawing on Tsing's metaphor of "friction" as the storied point of contact between lived realities and macro processes in global systems, I am also directed in my thinking on work, time senses, and everyday life by the idea of "rhythmanalysis," as suggested by Henri Lefebvre. Lefebvre spent a large portion of his career researching and thinking about daily life. He is most well known in English-speaking contexts for his work on space and everyday life (1987, 1991). However, in the last book he wrote, he focused on the interweaving of time as well as space with everyday life. In that book, the brief essay "The Rhythmanalytical Project" suggests an entire spatiotemporal terrain to be explored by subsequent "rhythmanalysts"— that is, scholars of the rhythms of everyday life. As Lefebvre observes, "The analysis of everyday life shows how and why social time is itself a social product" (2004, 73–74).

Lefebvre begins his essay with three hypotheses that serve as useful points of orientation as I discuss Benigno's, Maximo's, and my own senses of time, work, and everyday life. Lefebvre sees contemporary time senses as fusions of capitalist conceptions with other models of cultural organization. His opening hypothesis is that "first, everyday time is measured in two ways, or rather simultaneously measures and is measured. On the one hand, fundamental rhythms and cycles remain steady and on the other, the quantified time of watches and clocks imposes monotonous repetitions." His second hypothesis suggests that he sees this encounter not as a completed project but as a contested dialectic that results in strange and distorted experiences for social subjects: "Second, there is a bitter and dark struggle around time and the use of time. This struggle has the most surprising repercussions. So-called natural rhythms change for multiple, technological, socio-economic reasons, in a way that requires detailed research." This struggle, while an incomplete dialectic, results in a dominant time structure in the globalized world of contemporary capitalism. Time as quantified and partitioned becomes a generalized notion: "Third, quantified time subjects itself to a very general law of this society: it becomes both uniform and monotonous whilst also breaking apart and becoming fragmented. . . . These fragments form a hierarchy, but work remains to a large extent essential, the reference to which we try to refer everything else back" (2004, 74).

Lefebvre calls for detailed research on the specificities of transnational encounters and contests with capitalist temporality. This chapter revolves around issues of time as it relates to work and everyday life. As such, it is informed by the anthropological study of time in its various cultural conceptualizations; however, I am not attempting a direct study of concepts of time itself, so I do not focus on the fairly lengthy anthropological literature on this topic. For a full review of this literature up to the early 1990s, see the excellent article "The Cultural Anthropology of Time," by Nancy Munn (1992).

The historian E. P. Thompson, drawing on Lefebvre's work on the everyday, discusses a distinction between "task-oriented time" and the "clock-oriented time of industrial capitalism." With respect to the former, Thompson observes that

> three points may be proposed about task-orientation. First, there is a sense in which it is more humanly comprehensible than timed labour. The peasant or labourer appears to attend upon what is an observed necessity. Second, a community in which task-orientation is common appears to show least demarcation between "work" and "life." Social intercourse and labour are intermingled—the working-day lengthens or contracts according to the task—and there is no great sense of conflict between labour and "passing the time of day." Third, to men accustomed to labour timed by the clock, this attitude to labour appears to be wasteful and lacking in urgency. (1967, 60)

Thompson points out that the conversion of labor to "money" proceeds even in the absence of clocks and capital, as in the example of seventeenth-century English farmers who already had a well-established practice of accounting for labor in "dayworkes." Thompson argues that whenever labor is done for some entity other than the individual—even, for example, for an extended family—the process of converting labor into the currency of time is implied. The sense of losing control of one's time is the key here, according to Thompson: "Those who are employed experience a distinction between their employer's time and their 'own' time. And the employer must use the time of his labour, and see it is not wasted: not the task but the value of time when reduced to money is dominant. Time is now currency: it is not passed but spent" (1967, 61). Still, Thompson suggests that, even up to the early era of industrial cottage-based work and shopwork in the seventeenth and eighteenth centuries (and for some pursuits even to this day), work time was something changeable and flexible, given various tasks: "The work pattern was one of alternate bouts of intense labour and of idleness, wherever men were in control of their own working lives. (The pattern persists among some self-employed—artists, writers, small farmers, and perhaps also with students today, and provokes the question whether it is not a 'natural' human work-rhythm)" (ibid., 73).

PAST PREFERENCES OF SARAGURO WORK RHYTHMS

Saraguro work strategies have long revolved around raising food for family consumption, including plants such as potatoes, corn, beans, and much more, as well as animal products such as milk, eggs, and meat. In the past, growing and using food and fiber occupied much of the work time of Saraguro people, and even today families with sufficient and diverse landholdings spend a good portion of their working time on such agropastoral activities. Hard, physical work has traditionally been taught as an admirable value. Luis Macas describes life growing up under traditional arrangements in Saraguro:

> The child always has a chore. We were not playing. In this time there weren't toys. We would go to harvest, not corn, but *achochas*, or beans, and we had little baskets, and it seemed like play. But it was directed and we learned responsibility from a very young age. . . . My father had more than twenty-five sheep, and we had to take them to the hills, pasture them, and bring them home in the after-

noon. And our father taught us that while we were herding the sheep we shouldn't walk with an empty body. We had to gather grass for the guinea pigs or carry home firewood. We had to learn to carry, because if not, the body learns to walk around doing nothing. (Macas, Belote, and Belote 2003, 225)

This kind of dedication to the value of hard, physical labor serves as a guidepost, even for Saraguros, such as Macas, who have gone on to non-agropastoral careers. Macas, Belote, and Belote write,

> Those with traditional family upbringing become skilled at useful tasks at a young age, and they value these experiences highly. Adult responsibilities include care of the family, participation in community life, attention to religious life, and care of the animals and crops. Saraguros whose living is based in agropastoralism always seem to be busy with a lot of work to do. Even when visitors are present, the women spin or prepare a meal; the men weave or repair tools. Their bodies are seldom "empty." The lifestyles of the many Saraguros who have entered non-agropastoral employment as doctors, veterinarians, lawyers, teachers, office workers, and community development workers have undergone many changes, but most of them try to participate in agricultural activities whenever they can, even if only family and neighborhood *mingas* are involved. (Ibid., 225–226)

Resistance to the restrictions of wage labor has also been "traditional" to Saraguros, as Linda and Jim Belote observed during the 1960s and later described:

> First, when Saraguros work for other people they insist, where possible on doing so on a contract (piece-work) basis; they strongly dislike working for hourly or daily wages. One who works on a contract basis — say clearing two hectares of land, or weaving six meters of cloth — can accomplish the task more or less how and when he or she wishes to do so. Working for wages, however, assumes the participation of a "boss" who is concerned that an adequate amount of work be done for the money paid per unit of time. The boss in this situation will be much more concerned with giving orders, of being in a dominant position vis-à-vis the worker. Saraguros do not want any bosses around giving them orders. Pref-

erence for piece-work rather than time-based wages is probably common among people who place a high emphasis on personal autonomy. (Belote and Belote 1984b, 40)

The Belotes suggest that this level of desired autonomy traces to the fact that the Saraguros historically lived in a low-technology context, wherein all members contribute work to the household economy from an early age. They suggest that children learned the worth of their efforts early in life as they mastered their capacities for tending animals, caring for siblings, weaving, and other common daily activities. In addition, this pattern of work takes place in a seamless context with other aspects of daily life, so that work does not occupy a social or mental space different from other activities.

In this context, children are much more familiar with the adult working world—its difficulties and rewards, its problems and how they are solved—than are children in high technology societies where the worlds of childhood and of productive work are more rigidly separated. . . . Some work patterns themselves provide times of nonwork pleasure. For example, while caring for cattle in the high pastures, older children and young adults may take time to doze in the sun, to talk with neighboring herders, to play games, or to engage in courtship activities. (Belote and Belote 1984b, 42)

This lack of separation between the experiential spaces of work and daily life serves as one of the defining features of what I am calling *la vida matizada*.

TRANSNATIONAL IMMIGRANTS IN PURSUIT OF WORK
OPPORTUNITIES IN INDUSTRIAL AGRICULTURE

Maximo, after some time as a traveling, international musician, found work on a farm located in Chester (not its actual name), a town of about thirty-five hundred residents located in the upper Midwest of the United States. Created during the railroad boom of the 1870s–1880s as a speculative development by an investor from the East Coast of the United States, the town served primarily as a station along the train line between Chicago and Minneapolis–St. Paul. The community has long depended on agriculture for its economic existence. Its agriculture, from the beginning, has been linked to a larger economic sphere, providing food for city dwellers located elsewhere on the railroad line. By the early part of the twenty-first century, Chester, like most of the agricultural areas of the United States, had become fully incorporated into industrial agriculture, with large-scale confinement house dairy and poultry operations dominating the landscape. Thousands of acres of land are planted to monocrop fields of corn and soybeans. The resulting crops feed the animals held inside large complexes of barns and milking parlors.

In this context, the employment landscape has become decreasingly attractive to local residents. Transnational migrants, often from Mexico and Central and South America, increasingly fill agricultural labor roles. The place where Maximo works consists of three separate "farms"—complexes of buildings located in distinct clusters—with more than a thousand dairy cows living in warehouse-like, metal-sided buildings. The cows never leave the buildings, and workers usually live on the farm in housing provided by the owner.

According to a report by the Program on Agriculture Technology Studies (PATS) at the University of Wisconsin–Madison, immigrant workers account for about 40 percent of the hired labor force on Wisconsin dairy farms (Harrison, Lloyd, and O'Kane 2009). Of these workers, 88.5 percent come from Mexico, with most of the rest coming from Central and South America. My observations at the farm where Maximo works corroborate this study. Laborers now are nearly all Mexican or Ecuadorian transnational immigrants. Maximo said that when he first visited the farm in the late 1990s, many of the workers were local teens, with only a few immigrant workers. This shift away from U.S.-born workers was documented by the PATS study:

> Farmers we interviewed reported difficulties finding US-born workers willing to fill these new dairy farm jobs. Farmers said young people in rural Wisconsin have little desire to work on dairy farms, and that it is hard to find US-born people willing to work long hours, night shifts, and weekends. At the same time that dairy farmers need more employees and have a difficult time finding "reliable" local help, many people from other countries are immigrating to the United States in search of such work. (Harrison, Lloyd, and O'Kane 2009, 2)

The PATS study underscores the complexities of motivations for migration, including the fact that globalization has undermined the ability of people to remain in place in their home communities: "People migrate for many reasons. Some people migrate to reunite with their families or to flee war or other violence. Others migrate because their communities lack sufficient economic opportunities or because multi-lateral trade agreements (like NAFTA [the North American Free Trade Agreement]) have allowed for an increased flow of low-price commodities into other countries' domestic markets, thus undercutting domestic producers' ability to compete, and disrupting those rural economies" (ibid.).

Dairy farmers know they ask immigrant workers for hard labor and for lower wages than U.S.-born workers are willing to accept. In the words of two dairy farmers quoted in the report,

> It's not about Hispanics. It's about who wants to do the job. We don't get a lot of applications from people who want to do the job. There are lots of myths out there. . . . In our area you hear from some people that these people [Hispanics] are taking jobs away. But the fact of the matter is that there is nobody here who will work for those wages. The folks in ag cannot afford to pay those wages. (Harrison, Lloyd, and O'Kane 2009, 3)

Immigrant workers are concentrated on large farms. The study shows that immigrant workers account for 3,051 out of 9,236, or 33 percent, of workers on dairy farms with fewer than six hundred cows, but they account for 2,266 out of 3,316, or 68 percent, of workers on dairy farms with more than six hundred cows. As farmers have struggled with supplying agricultural products as bulk commodities to the industrial food system, they have been forced to adopt increasingly industrialized methods, such as round-the-clock milking. These changes rely, for various reasons, on a supply of workers from Latin America: "Many Wisconsin dairy farmers are pursuing a strategy of increased production to make ends meet or increase farm income, thus increasing the size of their herd and/or shifting to a three-times-per-day milking schedule. Both of these strategies require more workers" (ibid.). A primary outcome of these decisions by individual farmers is that an increasing number of people from Latin America who have lived largely as rural peasants with one sense of how work should be ordered and how their everyday lives should be lived are incorporated into a new system of labor and time. This system differs fundamentally from the rhythms of work and daily life that they have previously experienced. The result, a disjunctive experience of work as something separate from daily life, undermines the possibilities of living *la vida matizada*.

The University of Minnesota Duluth is a public university with approximately ten thousand undergraduate students, and a few graduate programs, located in Duluth, Minnesota. The community's economic heyday related to global capitalism was some decades ago — perhaps as far back as the 1920s, when income from timber and iron exploitation was at its height. The region has struggled to maintain a viable economy and stable population through various booms and busts based on resource extraction. Jobs at the university where I teach are locally considered to be excellent work opportunities because of high wages and good benefits in terms of the local economy. According to the City of Duluth (Hamre 2008), the median per year family income in the region is $58,900, which means that the $110,000 my wife and I combine in earnings puts us at almost twice the local median. At the time of this writing, the city of Duluth has a population of about 85,000, which is 25,000 fewer people than in the peak decades of the early twentieth century. Iron ore mined in the region has been used for industrial applications and consumer products sent all over the world, including, in all likelihood, products and applications in Ecuador. For example, a major global corporation, 3M, started in the region as Minnesota Mining and Manufacturing and has had offices and distribution networks in Ecuador since 1977.

According to standard review protocols in my collegiate unit, as a tenured professor I am expected to spend 50–65 percent of my time teaching, 25–40 percent of my time conducting research, and 10 percent of my time in service activities. My contract (achieved by faculty union negotiation) officially runs for nine months a year, although I have opted for my income (and the realities of the workload) to spread across the full year's calendar. For example, the original draft of this chapter was written in stops and starts in the summer of 2007 — a time when I am technically not under contract, but during which I have to hustle to complete research and writing, the part of my job that I do not have adequate time to complete during the semesters when I am teaching. I drafted this chapter while simultaneously working on two other intellectual projects and meeting the everyday demands of a family life full of the obligations of raising a young child and a teenager.

I make this observation of my work context to include in this analysis the rhythms of academic work — something that is usually intentionally elided or accidentally concealed from view in published articles and books. Academic life, originally modeled on masculine, monastic models of time and daily rhythms, is much messier in an era of post-feminist cultural realities, when the writing subject cannot be assumed to be a lone male whose sole responsibility is to complete "the work" of a tenure-track, monk-like professor. (For a comprehensive description of models of work, including chapters on work and the monastic movement and work in the modern world, see Applebaum 1992. For an interesting set of essays on the nature of academic life and work rhythms, see Pelias 2004.) With these three contexts briefly outlined, I describe the specific work rhythms of each of the men discussed in this chapter.

RHYTHMS OF WORK AND DAILY LIFE 1: "TRADITIONAL" SARAGURO TIME

Benigno begins his day early. Up before daylight at 6 A.M., he often starts his day with a brisk walk to the farm located along the river about two miles from his house. He waters the animals, moves their stakes to fresh grazing ground, and tends the chickens on a hillside above the river.

By 7 A.M., Benigno returns with the milk he has collected. He gives the milk to Ana Victoria, who boils it with an herb gathered from the gardens near the house, often *cedron* (lemon verbena) or *manzanilla* (chamomile). Breakfast consists of this hot milk and boiled plantains. Often when I am staying with Ana Victoria and Benigno, he has already had his morning meal and gone on to other chores by the time I rise, write morning notes, and join Ana Victoria and the kids in the kitchen. Some days Benigno makes an early run into town to gather materials for a project or to take his mother there.

While he is in town, Benigno runs errands for his family and serves as an informal taxi driver. In all the trips I have made into town with Benigno, he has never failed to pick up and drop off passengers and cargo throughout the town of Saraguro, each time collecting between ten and fifty cents per passenger. When the truck is moving, it is working, as Benigno reminded me one Sunday when we were in town for market. I had asked whether he intended to join his community's soccer team for a match. He eventually made it to the soccer match, but not before he had also run people and market purchases to three of the surrounding rural communities. Money-earning transport mixes fluidly and naturally with the rhythms of recreating and visiting with friends and acquaintances.

On nonmarket days Benigno returns perhaps by 9 A.M., where he finds me working on a necklace with Ana Victoria while sitting on the porch at the low table he built. Sometimes he will take a break to work on whatever necklace Ana Victoria has set out at her place. As a community storekeeper for the upper end of Tuncarta, as well as one of the best seamstresses, she often rises from the table to tend a customer at the store, collect a head of lettuce from the garden to sell to a neighbor, or work inside at the treadle sewing machine on a skirt or seam for a visiting neighbor. Benigno will sit for a while, teasing me about how much faster he is at beadwork and talking to the small children who are often around the house—both his own and the children of the neighbors.

Afterward, he turns his attention to whatever project he has under way. During one fieldwork session this was the creation of an orchard of *tomates de arbol* (tree tomatoes; *Solanum betaceum*). The field across the road had previously been planted in potatoes and other vegetables that had been harvested before my arrival. Benigno had been growing *tomates* plants from slips cut from his mother's adjacent orchard for about a year prior to preparing the ground for the trees. The planting will be large enough to provide Benigno and Ana Victoria with all the *tomates* they need, as well as provide major portions for his mother's household, with sufficient left for marketing. He chops the ground with a large hoe and prepares rows of two-foot high plant slips spaced about ten feet apart. He does not disturb the ground between the tree rows, which hosts an ongoing planting of peas, carrots, and cabbages. Benigno works for several hours on this task, often with the assistance of his youngest brother, Hernan, who lives nearby with their mother. They work steadily under the growing heat of the sun, and I continue working on the necklace and lose track of where they are and what they are doing. At one point I look up to see a neighbor working the adjacent ground with a team of oxen paired on a hand-hewn yoke. Benigno and his brother take a water break and chat with the neighbor for a few minutes.

Lunch, the timing of which depends on how close Benigno is working to the house, takes place between noon and 2 P.M. and generally serves as the largest meal of the day, with rice, a soup usually made with potatoes, cheese, fava beans or peas, and a salad, with the addition of a fried egg or (rarely) fried meat. The salty soup broth and juice and/or an herbal tea provide much needed hydration in the middle of the day, as the often dry mountain air and warmer afternoon temperatures sap moisture from active bodies.

In the afternoon, Benigno either returns to the orchard for a few hours, runs into town again, or takes up a new task. A few times a month he waters avocado trees in another small plot from a spring and chops away weeds from a circle about five feet in diameter around the trees. Benigno returns to the house several times in the afternoon to get tools or redirect his energies into other projects and often stops to chat. During one field-work session, when I took my twelve-year-old daughter along, he was drawn into playing whatever game my daughter was teaching his own daughter, such as hopscotch, or that my daughter was learning from his, such as a game involving a challenge to progressively do more complex bounce patterns with a small ball.

Afterward he disappears to visit the farm on the river again. Once when he returned, he was riding his horse because he planned to let his nephew use it in the morning to collect firewood from the mountain. Strapped to the horse's side was a branch cut from a type of coconut palm. The fruits do not grow large at this altitude, but there are clusters of small, green coconuts, about the size of walnuts in their husks, that can be cracked open with a stone to pry out the hard, white flesh. This branch sat in the yard, and for several days the kids would often stop to crack a few as a snack. Benigno and Ana Victoria, too, sometimes stopped to eat a few and socialize as they went about their work.

The evening meal, around 7 P.M., is usually less substantial than the midday meal—rice and perhaps boiled plantains and a salad. Sometimes we sit and swap stories, but often Benigno heads off to a community meet-ing or to join the soccer game in the lighted *cancha*, located a couple hun-dred yards down the hill. After a mixed and varied day of work, socializ-ing, playing, and eating, he finishes his day after 10 P.M., sometimes as late as midnight.

Occasionally Benigno's work rhythm varies from this general pattern. For example, during two seasons in 2006, totaling more than fifty days, Be-nigno's pattern varied on only eight days. Twice he traveled into the Sara-guro town center to assist a nonindigenous acquaintance. He was gone the entire day from dawn until after dark. Twice Benigno gave up workday ac-tivities to accompany his mother on day-long tasks—one time to travel to the large coastal city of Guayaquil to straighten out some sort of bureau-cratic issue, and another time to drive her to the city of Loja so that she could make market purchases. This latter trip was not really necessary, as his mother usually finds other transportation, but Benigno and Ana Vic-toria wanted to take me to see the large city that is closest to Saraguro.

Ana Victoria used the opportunity to scout for good prices on the black fabric she uses to make *polleras*, the inner skirts she sews and embroiders with beads for artisanal income. The hem of the *pollera* is embroidered or sewn with beads and peeks out underneath a pleated overskirt (*anacu*) of handwoven cloth.

The other four times, Benigno spent the bulk of his workday on proj-ects related to the construction of a house adjacent to his own that he and his brother-in-law Maximo are building together. I will discuss this joint project at more length, but first I want to describe the very different rhythms that Maximo experiences as a worker caught up in transnational labor opportunities.

RHYTHMS OF WORK LIFE 2:
GLOBAL-INDUSTRIAL TIME

Maximo works six days a week at a dairy farm in the community of Chester. The farm consists of several large confinement facilities for a herd of more than one thousand dairy cattle. The cattle spend their lives in various barns, corridors, and milking parlors. Workers milk the cows three times a day at eight-hour intervals and fill three different, round-the-clock shifts. Maximo began there as the primary worker tending the cows during birth. The farm employs approximately sixty workers, many of whom are Saraguros, but other workers are from Mexico and other Spanish-speaking countries.

The Saraguro connection began in the mid-1990s when Segundo, a Saraguro man, came to the United States to complete a master's degree in animal science. Segundo was already a certified veterinarian in Ecuador, but because of different requirements in the United States, he sought further education. Segundo worked at the farm on an internship related to his studies, subsequently becoming a manager of operations. The farm owner was so impressed with Segundo's work habits that he asked whether more Saraguros could come to work for him. Segundo, who has since moved on to create his own consulting business and his own dairy operation, became the nexus for a number of Saraguro workers to come to the farm.

The farm owner has been supportive of Saraguro people's efforts to seek labor in the United States, and now a number of Saraguro families have relocated to Chester. Maximo, on a resident worker visa, has legal permission to work in the United States, unlike many immigrants. For years he unsuccessfully petitioned for entry for his wife, Esperanza, and so he worked much of the year at the farm and returned whenever possible to visit his family, including his wife and small sons, in Ecuador. His employer valued Maximo's labor, so whenever Maximo left to spend time back home, his job remained available to him when he returned to the United States.

Maximo's work routine varies only slightly each day as he makes his rounds to check on equipment, workers, and cattle. He sometimes works a 6 A.M.–3 P.M. shift or a 3 P.M.–midnight shift. On days he works the morning shift, he rises at 5 A.M., dresses, and eats breakfast alone in the simple, functional structure the farm's owners have built for worker housing. Eighteen workers live in the building, which resembles a typical midwestern sheet-metal farm machine shed, but it is insulated, heated, and air conditioned and contains about ten double rooms, a single shower, and a kitchen area for cooking. The room Maximo lives in has two narrow beds, but he sleeps alone. The second bed serves as a couch for visitors.

After eating, Maximo crosses the road to one of the farm's main complexes and begins his workday. The regularity of his labor makes it easy to summarize in a few sentences. He punches the time clock and begins a repetitive routine of checking each milking unit for maintenance needs and consulting with shift workers, both the men who work in the parlor as milkers and the men who work in the barns as pushers, who move the cattle to and from the parlor. The cattle spend the rest of their days in open barn areas where they eat and rest. Sometimes Maximo repairs equipment, and sometimes he assists other employees as they need help. As part of his job, he visits the birthing barn, where he tends to the pregnant cows.

The routine is not physically taxing and rarely varies from this pattern. Maximo explains that in Ecuador the work he does often requires much more physical exertion and stamina but that he always ends a work shift at the farm more tired than after what might be a longer workday back home. In Tuncarta I have seen Maximo and other men spend many hours working at physically tough jobs such as planting, hoeing, or digging and then end the day after dark by playing soccer or volleyball for a few hours. In contrast, Maximo says that when he completes a work shift at the farm, he inevitably goes back to his room exhausted and ready to sleep.

This exhaustion stems, Maximo says, from being "head tired," a phenomenon that he attributes to the regularity and repetitiveness of the work and to the fact that he is required by company policy to do everything in prescribed ways. While Maximo expresses gratitude for the opportunity to earn what in Ecuador is considered a very good income, as well as contentment with the opportunity to learn new things and new ways of doing things, he also has a strong critical perspective on the "one-way-of-doing" orientation of the industrial farm where he works, as well as the way of organizing time at the farm.

"In my country we have many ways to do something, but here, just one," he says.

> Just do that, nothing else. That's what the administrator here is saying. [For example, at home] we use *palancas* ["handles"] for picking

up a cow. But we also know many other ways [to get a downed cow to rise]. Because we raise cattle there, and we imagine something to do. But here . . . here it is, "No, just take the skidsteer. With the skidsteer you can do it—nothing else." But we have many ways. They [the farm owners–managers] make a rule, and it's how we have to do that."

Maximo's words unpack a further elaboration of the *vida matizada* approach to life—an understanding that in any given situation there can be many ways to proceed rather than just a single, strict course of action. As a cross-cultural traveler, his awakened anthropological consciousness compares realities in different setting and results in a critical statement about the limited practices available in one of those settings.

Maximo's critique echoes that of thousands of shopworkers objecting to the routinization of work over the last few hundred years of increasingly industrialized models of labor under capitalism. His critique arises from a keenly felt, embodied experience of the fragmentation of daily life that is caused by transnational migration and subjugation to the work rhythms required by contemporary capitalism. Maximo has been traveling between his home in Ecuador and the United States for nearly twenty years, beginning in 1995 when he arrived on a cultural visa to play with a traditional Andean music group. Over the next several years, he periodically visited the United States to perform at festivals and universities throughout the Midwest and the East Coast. He visited the farm where he now works in 1995 and saw his fellow Saraguro, Segundo, begin as an intern and then become a regular worker at the farm.

When the farm's owner offered to help Maximo secure a work visa, he accepted. Most employment in Ecuador's economy, dominated by multinational oil centered in the Amazon and agricultural companies centered in coastal regions, was distant from his home and poorly paid. He received a few weeks of training in industrial cattle management at a workshop in California and began the pattern of working most of the year at the farm and traveling occasionally back home to visit. The decision to pursue this split life is not without repercussions for Maximo, his family, and his community.

At the community level, Maximo has served in the past as president, a task he is well suited to given his intelligence and natural leadership style. Community members have asked him repeatedly to serve another one-year term, and he would like to contribute his energies to community projects but has been unable to do so in light of his economically motivated travel. This pattern is common in communities affected by transnational migration—this is the infamous "brain drain" by which many of the most able and energetic individuals leave home for work.

At the personal level for Maximo, establishing a relationship with Esperanza, the woman he was dating at the time he began traveling transnationally, was difficult. They nearly broke up in the process, although they have subsequently married and work to make a life together despite the fact that Maximo spends long periods of time away from Ecuador. Their son—whom they named Aruni, which Maximo says is an Aymara word meaning "eloquent" (he found the name on an Internet site)—did not meet his father until the boy was nearly a year old. This adds to Maximo's weariness and his growing disillusion with his split life. He realizes that this life worked fine when he was young and had nothing specific to concern himself with back home, but now he can't do it anymore.

"It makes me head tired," he again observes, and he uses a metaphor to explain what his dual experience of work and time and everyday life is like.

"If you take a lion from its wild place in the mountains, and you bring it everything—nice foods and everything [including] water—but he's still not comfortable. We [immigrant workers] are thinking in two ways with the things we have to do here. That is what's happened."

RHYTHMS OF WORK LIFE 3: ACADEMIC TIME

As a college professor and researcher, I occupy a work schedule/time sense that contains affinities and disjunctions with the "traditional Saraguro" sense of time and work as *matizado*, or blended, with daily life, and with the "global/industrial" sense of time and work as hierarchical and separate from daily life. Lefebvre writes, "With regard to intellectual concentration and the activities with which it is bound up (reading, writing, analysis), they also have their own rhythm, created by habit, which is to say by a more or less harmonious compromise between the repetitive, the cyclical, and that which supervenes on them" (2004, 75).

During the academic year, I am expected to be on campus for a reasonable (in the industrial sense) number of hours. This includes preparation time, class time, office hours, advising students, attending meetings, working on committees, writing up research, and so forth. While there is no time clock for me to punch, the expectations of presence and time "at work" are made clear in myriads of informal ways—from department meetings scheduled at 8 A.M. to the comments of colleagues and administrators who might see me leaving the building at a time considered inappropriate: "Leaving early today, eh?" There is also much discussion among junior faculty regarding the "tenure clock," with the implied message that one must be diligently aware of a sense of work as tied to industrial models of time. These kinds of cultural mechanisms serve to remind me that I am working a "job" and that, as such, I should be subject to the organization of clock time, just as any industrial worker should be.

Yet much of the work I do takes place outside the borders of a "normal" workday: grading papers in the evening after my children have gone to bed, sometimes until midnight or later; reading texts and research books in the evenings or over the weekend, simply because that is when time is available; preparing second-semester classes during the winter holidays, when industrial workers might be expected to be taking time off. These are some of the ways that my relationship to work seems structured by time patterns other than the industrial one experienced by Maximo and other factory workers.

Then there is the "time off" during the summer that my friends who are not college professors envy. The work I do is seen as requiring much less overall time and effort to gain a professional salary than other kinds of work. One of my friends, a computer programmer, chides me with comments such as, "So, bet work was hard today. What'd you do? Put in two, three hard hours of reading, then called it a day?" This kind of teasing often silences me, not because there is truth in the specifics, but because it points to the fact that I have control over my time and workflow in ways that few workers in the contemporary global economy do. I am able to choose to work only a few hours during the regular workday and then spend the afternoon with my child or to cook a good meal for my family. Despite the fact that this may mean I work for four to six hours into the night, this flexibility is seen as an example of *la vida matizada* by my friends, and it is a freedom to be envied in a rigidly controlled world of work.

A colleague recently told a story about hiring a remodeler to add some shelving and to restructure her home office. Surprised to find both her and her husband home on a weekday morning, he asked what kind of work they do (they are both professors). Although they repeatedly explained that they work from home many times during the week, he called out "enjoy your day off!" as he left the meeting at their house. In an echo of Lefebvre's analysis of spatial aspects of daily life, the worker in this story could not accept the idea that a person's home can be a space of work. This contrasts directly with Benigno's experience of a *matizada* life in which "home" spaces and "work" spaces overlap and collapse into one another fluidly and regularly.

Time senses have been explored widely in the literature (Geertz 1973; Gardet et al. 1976; Fabian 1983). Lefebvre raises the question of whether there are characteristic traits of time that result in differential experience of everyday rhythms. He suggests a conception of what he calls "appropriated" time, which seems to be closer to the rhythmic pattern of Benigno's day as well as to much of the work I do as an academic, sharing a close affinity to the everyday rhythm of *la vida matizada*. Lefebvre writes:

> The time that we shall provisionally name "appropriated" has its own characteristics. Whether normal or exceptional, it is a time that forgets time, during which time no longer counts (and is no longer counted). It arrives or emerges when an activity brings plenitude, whether this activity be banal (an occupation, a piece of work), subtle (meditation, contemplation), spontaneous (a child's game, or even one for adults), or sophisticated. This activity is in harmony with itself and with the world. It has several traits of self-creation or of a gift rather than of an obligation or an imposition come from without. It *is* in time: it *is* a time, but does not reflect on it. (2004, 76–77; emphasis in original)

This analysis of appropriated time's character as uncounted because of the pleasing–absorbing–gifting nature of the activity being undertaken coincides with the idea of "blended time" and the "blended life" that Benigno and Maximo prefer. When I explained the idea of *la vida matizada* and how it appears to be an ideal for the way Benigno and the others in Tuncarta prefer to live, he agreed enthusiastically. Benigno embellished the idea by explaining that this blending is something "muy tradicional" to Saraguro people's sense of time and work and daily life.

Meanwhile, Maximo has grown increasingly discontented with the daily rhythms he experiences under the capitalist industrial model of time organization. When he is not working on the dairy farm, he dislikes the way that his only option is to dwell in the cold limbo of his over-air-conditioned, concrete-floored room. Lefebvre suggests that this negation of the body is fundamental to capital: "It [capital] constructs and erects itself on a contempt for life and from this foundation: the body, the time of living. Which does not cease to amaze: that a society, a civilization, a culture is able to construct itself from such disdain" (2004, 51–52).

The fragmentation of daily life and isolation of his body from social time has become so onerous to Maximo that rather than resting on his one day a week off from the dairy, he has found another job on a nearby horse farm where he cleans stalls, helps stitch harnesses that the owners sell over the Internet, and does other odd jobs. Lefebvre predicts this decision when he writes: "Capital kills social richness. It produces *private* riches, just as it pushes the *private* individual to the fore, despite it being a public monster. . . . So-called tribal, which is to say communal, forms of social life, have been ruined on a world scale" (2004, 53–54; emphasis in original).

When I asked Maximo directly about *la vida matizada* as an ideal, he agreed that he would prefer this style of life. He envies how his brother-in-law, because he is able to live such an everyday rhythm, is happy all the time. In contrast, Maximo characterizes his and his fellow dairy farm workers' own daily experiences while in thrall to industrial time as one that is *sufrido*, suffered, rather than lived.

RHYTHMS IN CONFLICT: BUILDING A HOUSE IN THREE DIFFERENT TIMES

On the second day after I arrived in Tuncarta, I helped Benigno and three of his friends move the concrete lid they had made to cover the hand-dug hole that serves as a septic pit for the plumbing in the house where I was to stay. Benigno had dug the hole and lined its rim with beams to support the heavy weight of the concrete he had poured to form a thick, square top. We grunted and heaved and put the thing in place, then climbed the hill to stand in the driveway and drink several beers that Benigno poured for us into a half-pint jar that we passed around. For the twenty minutes of work we did together, we got much more than twenty minutes of drinking and visiting.

The building of this house forms an arena in which the different time senses and rhythms of work experienced by Maximo, Benigno, and me rub against one another and create the kind of friction that makes things move and calls attention to something that needs to be pondered. As I have watched Benigno and Maximo build this house over the past few years, I have observed how these two men negotiate the friction-filled ground of different senses of time and work rhythms. This ongoing joint project underscores how time sense is not absolute but rather provisionally defined by all three men as each of us improvises strategies for economic subsistence.

Maximo and Benigno are partnering to build the house directly adjacent to the house that Benigno lives in with his wife and children. The older house belonged to Maximo's and Ana Victoria's father. Ana Victoria has inherited the use of it. Maximo, whose wife comes from another rural community, is building his own dwelling, which he also hopes to use as a hostel for visitors seeking cultural and ecotourist travel. The rhythms of my work as a visiting anthropologist have brought me here multiple times in the past eight years to be this hostel's first paying customer. While Maximo works in the United States, the two men have an informal agreement that when possible Benigno will work on the house. For each day Benigno works on the house, Maximo pays him $10. Maximo provides the capital input through his wage labor in the United States, and Benigno provides labor on the house as it fits with the other rhythms of his economic life. The arrangement offers mutual benefits, as Maximo invests some of his earnings abroad in a future place for his own living and Benigno earns cash for his work in an economy where other sources of direct income are not plentiful.

Friction arises, however, when the senses of time under which the men operate do not mesh. The friction comes between Maximo and Benigno as they consider how to prioritize their labor and capital regarding the house. Friction arises for me as I consider the fact that my presence in Tuncarta is literally the grit that changes people's priorities related to work. Before that first stay, Benigno had to drop the other work he was doing in order to make the place habitable for me to visit and pay for the room. Another point of friction emerges from the contrastive work experiences of the three of us. Maximo labors daily and repetitively in a cow barn to earn the capital to invest. Benigno moves between planting, hiking, watering, plowing, milking, hauling, and more, to create the life context into which I place myself, and as an academic my work appears to be in the realm of leisure, sitting at the kitchen table or the beading table and simply talking with and observing people.

Maximo sometimes complains that the work on the house does not progress as fast as he would like. He has the money to purchase materials, but the labor is not always forthcoming, as Benigno, operating in a more "traditional Saraguro" sense of time and labor obligations, attends to what he perceives as, in E. P. Thompson's term, *observed necessity* (1967, 60). That is, expectations within immediate social relations are more likely to convince Benigno that on a particular day he should fill his time with taking his mother to the market, or working with his brothers to prepare a field for planting *tomates del arbol*, or even taking a day-labor job to assist a wealthy townsman as he builds a new room on his own house.

The townsman encountering him on the street and seeking his labor is a more immediate social obligation that must be met with timely labor, lest an economic opportunity dry up. Benigno knows that whatever happens, his brother-in-law will still want his help on their joint project. In a sense, construction on Maximo's house is a form of "savings account" for future labor opportunities, but if Benigno does not immediately take up the offer from the townsman for work, that man will find another construction assistant, and the job will disappear from Benigno's matrix of economic opportunities.

The labor arrangements for the house highlight the tensions that arise as Benigno operates under a model of appropriated time and *la vida matizada* while Maximo would like him to operate under a model more akin to the clock time of industrial capitalism. My visits and the imperative to tap into another economic opportunity by providing me with a place to pay for room and board prompts a flurry of activity to get at least one room and a bathroom functional. The result of the frictions between the time senses of these men has been that Maximo, while continuing to envision this house as a future project for living and income, has begun to move the capital resources he accumulates from working under industrial clock time into other investments. He has purchased several parcels of land to increase his agricultural holdings. He has also bought an old house in the Saraguro town center, which he intends to repair and rent out for income. Because he has grown aware of the disjuncture between capitalist clock time and the appropriated time of *la vida matizada*, he has adjusted his strategy of converting cash into material assets that he will be able to draw on in the future in order sooner to end his own split existence. He says his goal is to return permanently to Tuncarta and take up the blended life rhythms that he longs for. He wants to punch off the time clock of industrial dairy farming and resume the rhythms of life of his home place. Having experienced both worlds and both ways of organizing work and daily life, he has consciously assessed which time he wishes to live within.

However, the choice is one shot through with hesitations and frictions. Tsing elaborates on the metaphor:

> Speaking of friction is a reminder of the importance of interaction in defining movement, cultural form and agency. Friction is not just about slowing things down. Friction is required to keep global power in motion. It shows us (as one advertising jingle put it) where the rubber meets the road. Roads are a good image for conceptualizing how friction works: roads create pathways that make

motion easier and more efficient, but in doing so they limit where we go. The ease of travel they facilitate is also a structure of confinement. Friction inflects historical trajectories, enabling, excluding, and particularizing. (2005, 6)

When Maximo and I drove on the roads through the Midwestern countryside surrounding the farm where he works in the United States, I asked him what he thought of the landscape and what he sees. He looked out over the regular rows of head-high corn and the straight, well-maintained roads and commented that there is a great deal of focused work that has been reified in the shape of the productive landscapes of the upper Midwest.

"We do not have this kind of focus in my country," he observed. "It is something we need to make our home . . ." and here he faltered for the word he wanted in English.

"Prosperous?" I offered. "More wealthy and able to provide work for the people of your home?"

"Yes," he agreed. "Prosperous. We need to keep our culture but learn from the good things we see in other places."

And with this, Maximo succinctly articulated the difficulty that people experience when they travel the pathways and routes that the globalizing world we live within creates and where we encounter ways of organizing life and the material world that differ from the usual ideas of our cultural context.

THE ENCLOSURE OF *LA VIDA MATIZADA?*

The critique of capitalist industrial time and work that emerges from this comparison is not new. Workers have lodged this kind of complaint against the demands of capitalist clock time for centuries, and social scientists and historians have been raising significant questions about how time is apprehended in industrial capitalist regimes for nearly as long. It is one of the characteristics of capitalism to reinvent itself along new lines that replicate old patterns, and hence it is necessary to constantly revisit emergent critiques that point out that "the more things change, the more they stay the same."

Thompson explores the historical development of an internalized time sense among laborers in industrializing, capitalist England and attributes a great deal of intentionality on the part of government and company policies designed to force workers into accepting the industrial sense of work time:

Thus enclosure and agricultural improvement were both, in some sense, concerned with the efficient husbandry of the time of the labour-force. Enclosure and the growing labour-surplus at the end of the eighteenth century tightened the screw for those who were in regular employment; they were faced with the alternatives of partial employment and the poor law, or submission to a more exacting labour discipline. It is a question, not of new techniques, but of a greater sense of time-thrift among the improving capitalist employers. (1967, 78)

Thompson's analysis provides a useful way to name the current struggles I see in my Saraguro friends over various senses of the time regimen best suited to living a good life. The act of training workers new to the industrial capitalist model of time and work is an act of *enclosure*, of privatizing what had previously been a common resource for the Saraguros, the sense of a balanced relationship between labor and other parts of daily life. What is unique to the situation faced by contemporary Saraguros, and indeed to workers in much of the world, is that the act of enclosure of the time sense is happening in fits and starts that are unequal across individuals, classes, genders, and communities. The same community, and even the same individual, accepts or rejects new work-time regimes unevenly, creating the kind of friction on the ground that Tsing describes. That friction creates opportunities for critiques at all levels of work, including in the home country of migrant workers, in the work environments they find in other countries, and in the academic writing that gets done around the experience of work time. Indeed, this conscription to a corporate capitalist model of time and work can also be seen in the academic world, where institutions such as Arizona State University and others have explicitly adopted a corporate capitalist model of organization that seeks to undermine the older time senses and rhythms of monastically modeled universities (Olson 2010).

While this chapter has focused on men's experiences in relation to labor and time, the experiences of women in the productive arena offers some similar examples. Using the key behavior of traditional, flexible schedules for household mealtimes among rural people, Mary J. Weismantel (1996) explores a similar enclosure process in the time sense of indigenous women in the community of Zumbagua, Ecuador. As men travel to urban areas for work and children attend schools with structured capitalist time regimens, women in Zumbagua are enclosed by a time sense that does not conform to the needs of an agrarian life. Where the norm had been four meals a day, spaced to allow long periods of uninterrupted daylight hours to attend to fields and animals, the urban-based, capitalist-inflected time regimen requires three meals, inflexibly scheduled. Weismantel writes:

> It is this kind of flexibility in mealtimes that is lost when rural people begin to bend to metropolitan rhythms. Work and time become more rigidly defined, and in the process, their meanings change. For urbanites, work, leisure, eating, cooking, child care, adult jobs, education, and "quality time" shared in the family are all sharply defined. With children in school and husbands gone to work, some Zumbagua women also are learning to separate these experiences. Time is not only altered because meals must be cooked according to the schedules of husbands and children; these schedules also create new categories of time, defined by the presence or absence of family members on the farm. (1996, 39)

Weismantel argues that while daily rhythms such as mealtimes may be forced to adapt to the enclosures of capitalist time, larger time patterns of indigenous life in the rural Andes based on agricultural cycles simply cannot, and so various forms of resistances arise to the enclosure of *la vida matizada*. Her book *Food, Gender, and Poverty in the Ecuadorian Andes* (1988) presents a nuanced description and analysis of how Zumbagua women negotiate their accommodations and resistances to the type of time enclosures I have been discussing here.

Many, perhaps most, workers in the global economy face a choice similar to that faced by workers in earlier industrializing eras: they must either accept the equivalent of underemployment and the metaphorical equivalent of the "poor law," in which families struggle for meager livelihoods, or submit to more exacting labor discipline. Many Saraguros, especially those who may not have adequate landholdings for subsistence agriculture, choose the more exacting labor discipline, and with this comes a forced acceptance that the bodies and experiences of individuals must submit to the dehumanizing effects of transnational migration in search of work.

In Benigno's fortunate case, owing to an adequate landholding for subsistence work and some access to cash income because of his brother-in-law's choice to submit to more exacting labor discipline, he is able to forge a third choice for himself, one that allows him to continue to live *la vida matizada*, a blended daily life full of diverse opportunities and activities. As for others like Maximo, who have chosen the more exacting path of industrialized labor time in foreign lands, it remains to be seen how resilient the Saraguros will prove to be. Can they continue to weave the necklace of daily life into a colorful, blended unity, or will the ruptures caused by migration result in something more like a watch chain, an everyday life structured by time fragmented and machined in a distant factory?

In the next chapter I discuss women's artisanal cooperatives, a creative way that some Saraguro women use to create economic opportunities that tap into transnational spheres without giving up a *vida matizada* existence.

A HOUSE IN THREE
DIFFERENT TIMES

*La arquitectura vernacula es una de las manifestaciones más
fehacientes de la adaptación del hombre en el medio ambiente.
Heredada de tradiciones milenarias, se fue acondicionando para
albergar al ser humano, proporciando ciertas comodidades que
estuvieron de acuerdo a las necesidades culturales. [Vernacular
architecture is one of the most authentic manifestations of man's
adaptation to the environment. Inherited from ancient traditions,
it was conditioned to house human beings, providing certain comforts
that agreed with cultural needs.]*

HERNAN CRESPO TORAL, INTRODUCTION TO
SARAGURO HUASI (TORAL 1990)

*Many Saraguros complained in the early 1970s about the lack of time
they had to work on their own projects during the house construction
season. Some Saraguros began to calculate that in overall terms,
combining outlays of cash, time, food and drink, present and future,
it is more desirable to build houses mainly with contracted (often nonindigenous) labor paid on a piece-work rate. As a result, some of these
people have attempted to remove themselves from the house building set
of obligation networks. They do this by using paid labor in their own
construction projects, and by manipulating their kinship networks in
a variety of ways.*

JAMES D. BELOTE, *CHANGING ADAPTIVE STRATEGIES
AMONG THE SARAGUROS OF ECUADOR* (1984)

*T*O ARRIVE IN ALMOST ANY COMMUNITY IN HIGH-
land Ecuador is to encounter a landscape in transition.
Many buildings seem perpetually under construction, as evi-
denced by sections of rebar jutting from cement second-floor
concrete pillars to await the day when available capital and
labor make possible an addition, even if that day is five years,
ten years, or a lifetime in the future. In Tuncarta the community center is in use but unfinished; the school has been under
construction since before I began visiting in 2005. Half-finished
houses of various styles and techniques dot the landscape, many

stalled in construction as their
owners gather resources, often
through transnational work.

Adobe bricks drying.

Maximo's house, which does
not strictly conform to traditional
Saraguro ideas about how a house
should be built, sits directly
adjacent to the house that his sister, Ana Victoria, inherited after
their father died. The inherited
house is made in the old style of
mud-brick adobe, while Maximo
is building a modern, fired-brick
house. Shiny roof tiles and new
bricks contrast with the lichen-
crusted roof and the mottled walls
of weathered, whitewashed adobe.

*The roofs of Maximo's
house (foreground) and
Ana Victoria's house.*

The house Maximo and Benigno are building occupies an odd location, culturally. No one lives fully in the house. It is imagined as a future home but also as a future economic opportunity. Maximo's travel for employment and my visits and stays in the house have turned it,

Front view of Maximo's house in 2009.

at least partially, into a zone of contact between the worlds of Tuncarta community life, transnational labor flows, and academic research.

The key benefit of getting the house built for Maximo lies in some future time when he will be able to dwell there and possibly earn income from paying guests. The key benefit for Benigno has been that he can earn some money while staying close to home and live a life in keeping with his preferences for *la vida matizada*, a life embedded in family, social relations, and varied work that he finds satisfying. Benigno spends his

As part of his work day, Benigno often assists Ana Victoria as she works on her beadwork and sewing.

Benigno adjusts the treadle sewing machine and will then work on stitching a blouse that Ana Victoria will embroider to be sold. His son and nephew watch.

Benigno weaves on a backstrap loom that hangs against the wall of the porch when not in use.

days in a fluid mixture of work projects that sometimes include working on the house he and Maximo are building but that also balances many other kinds of labor. He will sometimes set aside construction tools to help Ana Victoria with beading or sewing projects.

In contrast, for ten years Maximo has spent the majority of each year working at a dairy farm in rural Wisconsin. Because he has a legal visa for working in the United States, Maximo is able to visit home each year, unlike many Ecuadorians who seek work abroad through the expensive and dangerous route of unsanctioned immigration. He usually spends between four and eight weeks in Saraguro, visiting with his wife and children, renewing social ties, and cultivating his sense of self-identity as an indigenous Saraguro. His community misses his regular, sustained contributions to the social world. He served in the past as the president of his community and has been asked to do so again, but he knows he cannot do so unless he moves back to Tuncarta.

The house Maximo and Benigno are partnering to build has grown slowly. During my first visit in 2005, only one room was finished enough to use, and Benigno had to work quickly prior to my visit to ready a bathroom. Benigno often talks about what is proper to Saraguro traditions, and he acknowledges that a gas stove and refrigerator and indoor plumbing are not traditional. But he also accepts that these items make life a lot more convenient. His own kitchen

Benigno painting the newly replastered kitchen.

now has a full-sized gas stove that he and Ana Victoria purchased in 2009 after I brought about $500 to them that I had collected for selling Ana Victoria's beadwork in the United States to students, friends, and community members.

Benigno says he would like to build a second-story bedroom above the kitchen, so I can stay with him in the future, but the power company says he can't raise the profile of the house because it sits beneath the high-voltage transmission tower that Ana Victoria's father allowed to be built on his land in the 1970s. The transmission line carries electricity from distant power plants to and through the province. Ana Victoria and Maximo's father leased his property for placing a tower, and while the original house was "grandfathered" in and allowed to remain, Maximo may have to destroy, without compensation, his house because of the power line. He did not secure permits and has built in the area directly below the power line right-of-way. Ana Victoria and Benigno have

Maximo's house as seen from the slope below and from the window of my room.

been discussing building a new house on their land nearby, which is currently occupied by a small guinea pig shed built by Benigno's father sometime before the 1970s.

It is not unusual for family members to work together on house construction, as Benigno is doing with Maximo. In fact, the way large projects have traditionally been built is through a *minga*, or collective work party. Benigno and his brothers helped their brother-in-law build a house, where one sister now lives with her family. The brothers also built a house for another sister who lived for several years in Spain to earn the money to build a house. One house was built slowly because the first sister and her husband, neither of whom has traveled transnationally for work, had to save for years to purchase materials. In

Part of Benigno's extended family, most of whom live close to the house where Benigno and Ana Victoria live. From left: Marco, Petrona, Lara (with baby), Jairo, Nila (with the second of Lara's twins), Ana Victoria with Misael, Benigno, and Sauri. Petrona is mother to Marco, Lara, Nila, Jairo, Benigno, and another daughter, the mother of Sauri, who at the time of this photo was living in Spain for employment. Misael is the son of Benigno and Ana Victoria.

contrast, the house for the other sister, though larger, was completed relatively quickly because her work in Spain provided sufficient funds to pay for materials and to hire her relatives to work steadily on the project until it was completed.

Building a house can take months or years when economic resources are scarce. Here Benigno works with his brothers and brother-in-law to begin construction of a sister's house.

CHAPTER FOUR

Weaving la Vida Matizada

BEADWORK AND COOPERATIVES
IN SARAGURO WOMEN'S LIVES

Only if we are capable of weaving, only then can we make.

TIMOTHY INGOLD, "ON WEAVING A BASKET," IN
THE PERCEPTION OF THE ENVIRONMENT (2011)

*Andean gender relations have been associated with notions of
complementarity, where the male and female elements are viewed as
different, yet equally vital. The work that men and women do may
be different (men plow and women sow, for example), but each is
necessary for the survival (both actual and spiritual) of the group.*

ANN MILES AND HANS BUECHLER, INTRODUCTION
TO *WOMEN AND ECONOMIC CHANGE* (1997)

*I*N DECEMBER 2005, I BEGAN LEARNING SARAGURO
beading. The anthropologist Linda Belote arranged for me
to stay with Ana Victoria, an excellent artist who had previously taught
U.S. beadworkers at a workshop organized by Linda and the bead artist
Ann Severine. Ana Victoria showed me the beginnings of the *flores* pattern
using some of the beads I brought. When she tried to sew some of her own
beads into the petals, the technique didn't work because the beads I had
brought were smaller than the ones she buys in town. Many times over the
next month we talked about the differences in quality, colors, sizes, and
styles of the beads I had brought from home.

She showed how to make the *viga*, or base row, for a necklace in the
oldest pattern, *de colores*, which is simply alternating rows of different

colors. The women consider it the most traditional and authentic pattern; when they want to dress in what they called "proper" traditional manner, they wear only *de colores* necklaces. This would have been a logical way to combine colors as Saraguro women first started making necklaces around the middle of the twentieth century. They would not have been certain to have enough of any one color to serve as a background.

To bead, Ana Victoria set out a low table on the porch and covered it with a cloth. We sat on small benches to work. She pinned her work to the cloth to keep it secure so it wouldn't go flying and scatter beads and to keep it from twisting. Her hands moved quickly to pull stitches into place. A younger woman named Gladys worked with us. Ana Victoria said Gladys's mother, who lives nearby, was sick, so Gladys needed to earn money to help them live. She worked with Ana Victoria to learn to bead better and faster. She worked on making a replica of a rainbow pattern (*arco iris*) necklace that I had bought from a Saraguro vendor in Quito. The pattern, one of several versions of a model called "little sticks" (*palitos*), uses short, straight strings of beads to connect two woven sections.

While we worked, a visiting neighbor boy stumbled and fell against a wall. He wasn't seriously hurt, but he looked to each of the adults as if wondering whether he should cry. Ana Victoria said "Duro! Duro! Duro!" ("Hard!" or, more colloquially, "Tough!") while slapping the back of one hand against the other palm. He shook off his scare and wandered off to play.

Another woman, Carmen, came by after we had been sitting for about thirty minutes. I complimented her necklace, a large one with various shades of green against a black background—and she just said, "Hmm." She made the same noncommittal sound to several things that I said or that were said about me, prompting Pricila (Ana Victoria's daughter) and Gladys to make fun of her. Eventually she asked Ana Victoria to work on a *pollera*, an underskirt meant to be worn beneath a heavier outer skirt called an *anacu*. Ana Victoria took the skirt—a synthetic cloth that was a deep purple color—got her measuring tape, and marked the cloth with chalk. After a small nip with a scissors, she simply ripped the fabric in a straight line along its weave rather than cutting it—a sudden motion that startled me as I was focusing on my base row. Ana Victoria rose from her seat and went inside. I heard the treadle on the sewing machine a few minutes later.

Carmen (who is Ana Victoria's cousin) took Ana Victoria's seat and worked on the necklace Ana Victoria had begun with red, iridescent (*torna sol*) beads I had brought as a gift. After a brief discussion over how best to proceed on the necklace, Carmen had deferred and accepted the way

Ana Victoria wanted her to do it. We all beaded, with Carmen and Gladys sometimes talking to me, sometimes whispering to one another. They looked several times at the example of *arco iris* that I had brought to plan how Gladys would do her copy of it. At one point I heard Carmen whisper to Gladys, "What is it worth?" as if she didn't want to talk to me.

"Ask him," Gladys said and shrugged.

"I don't remember for sure, but I might have paid $16 for two necklaces," I said.

"So little?" Gladys said in surprise. "These are large for so low a price!" I thought more carefully.

"Perhaps I paid $16 for the larger one, and $11 for the smaller?" I said. They agreed that this seemed much more likely.

Ana Victoria completed the skirt while we beaded. In the time it took me to finish the base row, she had sewn a piece of flowered cloth along the hem of the skirt and cut a scalloped edge along the hem. The air grew misty as a damp breeze rolled down the mountain, and Ana Victoria shivered and hugged herself.

"Cha-chi!" she exclaimed—a Quichua equivalent for "Brrr!" She also observed, in Spanish, that the afternoon had grown *feo*, or ugly. Around 6 P.M. we moved inside as it grew dark and even colder.

CRAFTWORK AS ECONOMY IN SARAGURO

For at least twenty years Ana Victoria has depended on craftwork for her life. First and foremost this has been an economic dependence, as she has produced craft items and clothing to help meet the economic needs of herself and her two children and husband. Benigno and Ana Victoria estimate their cash income at between $2,500 and 3,000 per year, and about $1,800 of that comes from her beadwork, embroidery, and sewing. Ana Victoria's story may be a bit out of the ordinary, but only for the intense degree to which she focuses on artistic production. All women of Saraguro contribute significantly to their household economies, through combinations of cultivation of food staples or marketable produce, income from crafts, and other work. Each woman possesses a variety of artistic competencies, such as beading necklaces, making their distinctive black outer skirts, embroidering the hems of underskirts, spinning, knitting, or crocheting. Women also increasingly work as professionals such as teachers, restaurant managers, nurses, and more. Inheritance conventions in Saraguro tend toward both men and women receiving property. Indeed, Ana Victoria and Benigno have sufficient resources for subsistence agriculture because, in addition to his land resources, she brought both a house and fields into their marriage after inheriting them from her father.

In addition to pursuing economic benefit, however, Ana Victoria and many other women craft a *cultural* identity out of their handwork. Ana Victoria strongly feels her connection to this identity, and many of the people of her community recognize her for it. Both she and Benigno are proud of her distinctive work and consider it to be in keeping with the handcraft traditions of their ancestors. She is an unofficial teacher of many women in the community, and spending an afternoon with her at the beading table on her front porch reveals a constant stream of women stopping by with questions about beading, sewing, knitting, or embroidery. She patiently assists anyone who comes for help. Sometimes they pay her for some sewing, but most often she freely helps them get past a problem or make a design decision, and they go on their way.

This spirit of sharing and community characterizes many of the women's cooperatives that have formed in the Saraguro communities over the last few decades. These cooperatives, while providing economic opportunities, also serve critical social functions for strengthening intra- and inter-community solidarity, as well as providing an arena for practices that the members see as important to maintaining their cultural identities as indigenous women.

Gender in the Andes in general and in Saraguro in particular, as in any society, is complex and fraught with dynamics of power, daily practice, work, desire, control, and more. Irene Silverblatt reminds us of this in her study of gender ideologies and class in Inca and colonial Peru: "The experience of growing up female or male in Andean society is inseparable from the practical activities by which men and women reproduce their lives. And these activities, in turn, are indebted to the cultural meanings through which Andean peoples constructed identities of gender — constructed Andean women and men" (1987, 3).

My encounter with Saraguro culture and practices began with beadwork, which is primarily, though not exclusively, a female domain. Ana Victoria and the other women of the community use the practice of artisanal work as a crucial part of their attempts to weave *la vida matizada* for themselves as they contribute to the economic well-being of their households.

WOMEN'S ROLES IN ANDEAN SOCIETY: COMPLEMENTARITY, NOT HIERARCHY

As suggested by the second epigraph at the head of this chapter, Andean societies have not traditionally had a strong hierarchical division between the value of men's work and the value of women's work. Numerous studies of communities throughout the Andes highlight a basic parity in the valuation of men's and women's work (Bastien 1978; Belote 1978; Harris 1978; Isbell 1978). A weak separation between spheres suggests another manifestation of *la vida matizada*. Rather than a sharp distinction between the value of male and female work, the ideal relationship between the economic contributions of men and women sees the two as complementary and blended. In their introduction to an edited volume on women and economic change in the Andes, Miles and Buechler write: "Adapted to an agrarian lifestyle, the Andean tradition demonstrates a weak separation between the domestic/private and public spheres. Thus, the differential valuing of public (wage-earning) and private (domestic) work does not occur" (1997, 2).

Benigno highlighted this complementarity one afternoon after we had finished filming Luz Macas explaining how she spins thread. She sends finished thread to a male-operated weaving studio to be made into cloth. The cloth returns to her household, where she does the sewing, combing, felting, and dyeing that turns the cloth into woolen shawls. Benigno explained that women do the spinning and men do the weaving so that each sex will have a required and complementary role in the making of essential garments.

Lauris McKee (1997) points out that the weakness of this separation moderates patriarchal power within an indigenous family. Social conventions of property ownership also bolster the position of women:

> Contemporary ethnographers studying indigenous Andean communities inform us that patriarchal power within the traditional family is limited and moderated not only by customs and ideals, but by the leverage women's economic contributions give them in spousal negotiations. Women generally bring property of their own into marriage; if they decide to end the relationship, their husbands lose access to that property and to the labor-exchange relationships established with a wife's kin. In the subsistence economy, success in food production and handicraft manufacture is synonymous with wealth. Both sexes are major players in exchange networks in which labor, food, and craft items are the primary mediums. (1997, 15)

McKee cautions, however, that while complementarity in economic arrangements provides women with a measure of equity within the household, it does not always translate to political or ritual equality for women. While I observe many women in Saraguro making significant contributions to the economic well-being of their households through agricultural and handcraft work, it is also true that relatively fewer women than men occupy positions of political power in their communities. Women do sometimes run for and get elected to political office, but this happens far less frequently than would be the case in an equal society. This could be seen as analogous to the situation in U.S. society, where we claim equality between men and women but where, in fact, men maintain control over much of the political power and women's wages for the same work average only three-fourths that of men. In Saraguro, this inequality of presence in politics and economics likely stems from the history of Ecuador as a male-created and male-led nation-state, with electoral politics and economics derived from the patriarchal model of power brought to the Andes by the Spanish conquest and inherited by development agencies (as discussed in the next section below). In indigenous Saraguro, however, the domestic sphere of labor does not suffer denigration, as is often the case in the United States; rather, it is seen as significant by both men and women.

Ana Victoria entered her marriage with her own property, including the house the family now lives in and several parcels of agricultural land. The combination of her property with that inherited by Benigno makes it possible for the two of them to subsist without having to leave the community, something many other Saraguro people have had to do as families grow and landholdings become insufficient to support everyone. Ana Victoria's situation corroborates McKee's following observation: "The Andean case offers support to many authors who contend that women's equality of status is correlated with the degree to which they control resources the society values and the extent to which they are recognized as significant economic contributors" (1997, 16).

Ana Victoria and Benigno have a remarkably equal relationship, with both apparently having strong input into economic and other decisions for the family. Indeed, the families who appear to thrive the most in the community tend to have economic resources from both the woman's and the man's inheritances. The women of the community are also actively working together to build new economic opportunities for themselves and each other, regardless of inherited resources. A primary means for such opportunity building is the women's cooperative.

Development efforts by outside agencies in Saraguro offer an interesting study in the "success of failure." Linda Belote and Jim Belote (1981) called their article about such development efforts in the 1950s–1970s "Development in Spite of Itself: The Saraguro Case." The Belotes saw that development agencies usually come with agendas set in distant places, with little attunement to the cultural arrangements and needs of local peoples. For example, a UN-supported agency called the Andean Mission arrived in Saraguro in the 1960s. It eventually came under control of the Ecuadorian government as part of the Ministry of Social Projects. Throughout the 1960s and into the early 1970s the mission tried various development schemes set by priorities from the distant capital of Quito. These projects included latrine construction, training in the use of sewing machines, carpentry training, agricultural projects, and more. For various cultural reasons outlined by the Belotes in their article, these projects met with limited material success.

The Andean Mission attempted to use an existing traditional leadership structure that historically had limited scope. Each community had up to three leaders (*mayorales*) with limited power to call communal work parties to maintain trails and bridges. Aside from this function, each *mayoral* served primarily as a consultant and advisor to those in the community who felt inclined to seek advice. The Andean Mission attempted to use these community leaders to call cooperative work parties for a variety of tasks not normally seen as within the purview of these offices.

It is worth noting that the *mayorales* the Andean Mission attempted to work through were exclusively men and that the attempt to invest additional development authority in these male figures echoed exactly the process by which the Incas and then the Spaniards administered their empires:

> As the Incas tightened their grip over others, the imperial ideal of Andean malehood increasingly became the norm. Not only imposing or re-enforcing this definition with every married man on the tribute rolls, the Incas also asserted it as new positions in government emerged. The association of men with conquest and arms helps explain why the Incas appointed men to the new positions of power which developed with the expansion of empire. ... In keeping with royal gender norms, the Incas, who governed through a system of indirect rule, tended to confirm headmen as

links between conquered *ayllus* [communities] and the bureaucracy
of Cuzco. The power brokers of the empire were male. (Silverblatt
1987, 15–16)

The Spaniards used a similar approach, focusing on male authority figures
in trying to control the native populations of the Andes.

When the Andean Mission, even with good intentions, entered Saraguro and duplicated this gendered approach, they ignored a context in
which women's labor was significant and necessary for getting anything
done. Like earlier colonial efforts, they disregarded and diminished a preferred distribution of power in local communities. This predictably led to
an erosion of support for the mission's work:

> Through the 1960s support for the Andean Mission began to
> dwindle on the part of some of the *mayorales* and the community
> members. The Andean Mission tried to get the *mayorales* to blow
> their *quipas* [bullhorns] to call people to meetings and to *mingas*
> [work parties] for digging wells, building latrines, and making irri-
> gation canals, areas outside the *mayorales* traditional ken. For some
> who complied, it weakened the influence they once had held. Some
> *mayorales* declared themselves "enemies" of the Andean mission.
> Many community members began to ignore the *quipa*, even for trail
> *mingas*, which were, in their minds, being called much too often.
> (Belote and Belote 1981, 463)

While the Andean Mission's specific approach and projects often did
not lead to concrete development success, one arena where these efforts
took root and began to exert significant influence on Saraguro culture
was in cultivating the idea that it might be valuable to coordinate community efforts beyond kin networks for various objectives. Belote and
Belote write: "At the time of the initiation of their [the Andean Mission's]
work the indigenous communities had only a loose organization beyond
the family unit" (1981, 462). The Belotes later observed that, while the
mission did not actively incorporate Saraguro people into the decision-
making process for its projects, the people did see the value of holding
meetings to discuss and coordinate community efforts.

In fact, Saraguros began to hold community meetings independently of
the ones organized by the mission, something the mission saw as secretive
and threatening. At these private meetings, communities began to make
collective decisions regarding resource use:

At one secret *cabildo* [community council] meeting the use of some community-owned land in a forested mountain area nearby was discussed. It was decided to clear a certain amount of land and rent it out as pasture to members of a rural *blanco* community located in an adjoining *parroquia* [parish]. In this way their community would gain funds which could be used in any way the people decided. A large, well-attended *minga* was arranged to get the work done. (Ibid., 465)

The Andean Mission saw this kind of organizing as a threat, but in the long term, it suggests that the Saraguros learned the value of an innovation (community organizing around resource use) introduced by outsiders and adapted it to their own perceived needs. The Andean Mission ceased operating in Ecuador in 1973, but the Saraguros developed their own ideas for extrafamilial organizing. Women's artisanal cooperatives emerged over the next decades as one significant type of ongoing innovation for organizing.

LA COOPERATIVA TERESA DE CALCUTA

Each cooperative has its own distinctive history and composition, ranging from cooperatives with members from a single, small rural community to cooperatives with members from many rural communities as well as the city center of Saraguro. I have individually interviewed all members of La Cooperativa Teresa de Calcuta (the cooperative to which Ana Victoria belongs). I have also individually interviewed Zoila Chalan, leader of another cooperative (CEMIS — Centro de Mujeres Indígenas Saraguros), and Flor Cartuche, director of Warmipak Wasi (Quichua, meaning "Women's House"), a women's advocacy center and shelter that operates a craft cooperative to support the center's work. I also conducted group interviews with members of three cooperatives, including CEMIS, another group called Ñawpak, and another called Construyendo Nuevo Camino (CNC).

Since 2009, with the energy and support of Linda Belote and the Santa Fe International Folk Art Market, the cooperatives have joined together to form La Mega Cooperativa, which meets regularly to plan how each smaller cooperative can contribute to building larger markets for all of the groups.

Las Mujeres de Teresa de Calcuta cooperative (or Las Calcutas) consists of eighteen members, all of whom live in the rural community of Tuncarta. They chose the work of Mother Teresa of India as a model and inspiration for their group because they admire her advocacy for the poor and, especially, for women. Indigenous women of the community constitute the majority of members, but several nonindigenous women who live in Tuncarta also participate. For example, the former group president, Ana Lucia Chillogalli Mora, is a nonindigenous woman who moved to Tuncarta from the city of Cuenca after she married a nonindigenous man from the community. The current (2013) president, Maria Elena Sarango, is another nonindigenous woman.

Rosa A. Medina, matriarch of a large indigenous family, and one of the founders of La Cooperativa Teresa de Calcuta, provided the history of the group. The description that follows of the group's founding and history emerged over several informal discussions and one recorded interview with her.

The first cooperative of women in the community organized in 1976 as a group of mothers who met weekly to receive food aid and prepare a collective meal for their children. This group began to arrange programs and activities for their children and to work together to embroider blouses to sell. This effort resulted in a structure for cooperative organizing that has endured in the community, as the current women's group traces its history to the mother's group. Today the women meet weekly to work collectively on artisanal products that will be sold. The group collectively owns earnings from the sales. They make all decisions by consensus.

The women's group in the 1970s coordinated efforts with several development organizations from outside the immediate community, including a social pastoral mission from the city of Loja (about two hours away by bus) that brought used clothing to the women. Working with this outside organization gave the women assistance and experience in organizing themselves, though it did not focus on creating a market for their products.

The Tuncarta group had been operating in this manner for about half a decade when the Ministry of Agriculture began to use the community's existing social forms to distribute seeds and information. The Tuncarta women's group received seeds of cabbage, carrots, lettuce, and other vegetables. This government program lasted from about 1980 until 1985, with the goal of helping the women create kitchen gardens to improve the diets of their families. Ana Victoria and Benigno still grow many of their own vegetables of this kind. Some families (but not Ana Victoria and Benigno) still save and replant seeds from these vegetables. Rosa A. Medina reports that the one effort at development initiated by the government—

pig raising—was not particularly effective and was abandoned when the women realized that the cost of feeding the animals for market exceeded the amount to be made from selling them.

The group continued to exist in a low-level form even after the government no longer distributed seeds, but the women grew tired of maintaining it and it fell relatively dormant during the 1990s. In 1998, some of the women of Tuncarta, several of whom had been too young to participate in the older group, began to reorganize, and their energy coalesced in 1999–2000 to create La Cooperativa Teresa de Calcuta. The earlier women's group had attempted some work in creating economic opportunities but had not built substantive income for the women involved. In contrast, the renamed group is one of several such cooperatives in the indigenous communities of the area. The work of each cooperative focuses on the women who are its members. The Teresa de Calcuta cooperative enhances economic opportunities but, perhaps as significantly, provides an arena for the women of Tuncarta to strengthen their social solidarity and cultural identities during a time of cultural flux brought on by increasing participation in globalized cultural and economic systems.

Each member of the Calcutas must deposit two dollars a month into the "bank" created for the group. Since 2000 they have built a pool of money that they use for various purposes, but primarily as lending capital. Each woman may borrow money from the fund as needed and as money is available. The borrower pays back the loan with a 2 percent per month simple interest. These are advantageous terms compared to rates from local moneylenders, who charge interest rates in the double digits, if they lend at all. The woman who borrows may use this money to invest in equipment, such as a sewing machine to increase income, or to meet other financial needs and exploit other opportunities. Ana Victoria, for example, has borrowed money from Las Calcutas' fund to purchase an additional half hectare of land for her family. Benigno has planted avocado and *tomates de arbol* saplings on this land, to provide food for themselves as well as avocados to sell in the market.

Aside from offering this lending capital, the cooperative either provides or hopes soon to provide two other tangible benefits to its members: the use of sewing machines for the making of blouses and skirts and a place to use them. The machines and supplies purchased by the group currently reside in one member's house, but the long-term goal is to build a community center that will serve as a meeting- and workplace for the women. Each week they meet to work on crafts, including embroidery and beadwork. The pieces they complete during these weekly four-to-six-hour meetings are sold in Saraguro, at craft markets in other Ecuadorian cities, and abroad. The women have raised enough money to buy a plot of land near Tuncarta's center. Now they are working to earn enough to purchase materials and hire builders to coordinate the volunteer labor they and their families are ready to contribute.

Members of other cooperatives confirm similar historical trajectories rooted in both local initiatives and regional and national nonprofit and governmental efforts. Construyendo Nuevo Camino, located in the community of Kiskinchir, has an unfinished building that was initially funded by the government. The women of this cooperative tried for several years to raise rabbits as a commercial venture, but they say that the climate of the area is not conducive for the rabbits to thrive. When outside support dried up, the project ended. They now use the partially finished building only sporadically, primarily for meetings, but they hope to raise sufficient funds from craftwork to complete the structure as a women's community center and an eco-/cultural tourism lodge.

Variability of purpose and success for cooperatives resulting from fluctuating support by governmental agencies has been characteristic of rural cooperatives in recent decades. Vargas-Cetina, discussing the context of declining Mexican government support and regulation of rural cooperatives, writes:

> Today, grassroots organizations change rapidly in size, orientation, form, legal status and membership, responding to their changing economic, political, social and even religious contexts. Furthermore, as activists and NGOs increasingly take over tasks that used to be associated with government programs, the personal attitudes and values of people in key positions as advisers make a mark in the ways the organizations are structured and function. . . . Since, under the climate of neoliberal policies the state has largely withdrawn from many areas where it was once important, these individuals have become crucial. In the case of commercialization cooperatives, their time and trade horizons now coincide with the market potential of their products, which sharply rises or falls and is beyond local control. (2005, 230)

The Saraguro cooperatives depend heavily on the tastes and desires of people far from their communities. As Vargas-Cetina suggests, key advisors have been critical to the growing success of Saraguro women's cooperatives as they access markets in other countries. The Saraguros have long had important advocates in the transnational arena in the work of Linda and Jim Belote, who met in Saraguro when they served together in the Peace Corps in the early 1960s. The Belotes each went on to write dissertations in anthropology (L. Belote 1978; J. Belote 1984) about the Saraguros. They have also returned regularly and serve as friends, advisors, and students of all things Saraguro.

Linda, in cooperation with the bead artist Ann Severine, also serves as a crucial cultural broker (Kurin 1997; Causey 2000) to help Saraguro women build their cooperatives and to incorporate the work of these cooperatives into the transnational economic opportunities provided by the Santa Fe International Folk Art Market. Through the work Linda and Ann do on behalf of, and in conjunction with, the women of the cooperatives, the Saraguros earn between $5,000 and $15,000 per year for their communities. Since 2005, the cooperatives have successfully sent their work to be sold at the Santa Fe International Folk Art Market held annually in July. The market, produced annually by the Museum of International Folk Art, marked its tenth year in July 2013, with about one hundred and ninety vendors from nearly sixty countries. Collectively, the artists take home more than two million dollars each year for their work (Cerny 2011). The growth of crucial alternative trade networks for artisans is a topic unto itself, explored by several authors in an edited volume published by the University of Arizona Press (see Grimes and Milgram 2000).

Linda meets regularly with the Saraguro cooperatives to discuss arrangements, advise on designs to be produced, assist in the application process, and provide cultural translation between the Saraguros and the market. In addition, she advocates for the Saraguros with organizations such as the UNESCO Award of Excellence for Handicrafts program. Through these efforts she has helped both to build international recognition of the quality of Saraguro artisanal work and to support rising cultural self-confidence within the Saraguro community.

Linda and Ann work together to complete the artist's application and to secure permission for a woman from Saraguro to travel to the United States to represent the cooperative. Given the unequal relations of power and economics, this process can be quite involved. When Ana Victoria sought to travel to the United States in 2010 to represent Las Calcutas, she had to travel to the consulate in Guayaquil to secure a travel visa to the United States. To get such a visa, she had to show the letter of invitation from the market, show her marriage certificate, show that she had several thousand dollars available in a bank account, and more. Her first request was denied. An excerpt from the rejection letter reads:

> We regret to inform you that Mrs. Sarango was unable to qualify
> for a non-immigrant visa under Section 214(b) of the Immigration

and Nationality Act (INA). . . . To be approved for a visa, applicants must demonstrate to the interviewing officer that they are entitled to the type of visa for which they are applying and that they will depart the United States at the end of their authorized temporary stay. This means that before a visa can be issued, applicants must prove strong social, economic and/or family ties outside the United States.

Only after Ana Victoria compiled additional materials, including letters of support from a U.S. senator, was she finally granted a visa to travel to the United States.

In contrast, when I travel to Ecuador, I do not have to do anything more than make sure I have a current passport, then buy my ticket. The uneven frictions of contemporary globalization favor me and other travelers from wealthy nations as compared to people from less wealthy ones.

Once the women get to Santa Fe, they take a place alongside hundreds of artists from dozens of other countries as they try to earn income from their artistic pursuits. Linda and Ann serve as primary consultants, organizers, cashiers, and translators for the Saraguro women who travel to the market. The booth, designed originally by Ann Severine and developed over the last several years in conversation with each of the Saraguro women who have visited, draws visitors in with an overwhelming display of hundreds of works of wearable, beaded art. Ann's additional brokering activities include speaking to U.S. groups about Saraguro beadwork and selling Saraguro beadwork and bead patterns (see www.annseverine.com). Ann uses half of the proceeds from pattern sales to offset the costs for the cooperatives to attend the Santa Fe market, and she also solicits donations to Saraguro cooperatives from organizations such as the San Diego Bead Society.

The cooperatives in Saraguro with coordinating help by Linda Belote and the Santa Fe International Folk Art Market have combined to create La Megacooperativa Saraguro with the goal of creating still greater opportunities for the women. In 2013, after close to a decade of attending the direct-to-consumer market in Santa Fe, the Saraguro Mega was selected as one of only twenty vending groups to offer their work at a wholesale market in Dallas, Texas. This could potentially lead to a larger and more steady stream of work for the women of La Mega. The folk market coordinated efforts to create a stunning catalogue of the women's work, which can be found on La Mega's website (www.lamegabeadwork.com).

Meisch (1998a; 1998b, 149–153) traces the long history of Ecuadorian bead use, which dates to pre-Hispanic use of seeds and beads made
from the shell of the spiny oyster (*Spondylus princeps* and *Spondylus calci-
fer*), other bivalve mollusks, and various other materials such as bone, clay,
stone (various types), and metal. People have used such beads throughout
Ecuador for a considerable length of time, as far back as the Formative
period (more than 2000 B.C.E.) and running through the pre-Hispanic,
colonial, and modern eras to current times. The gender and ethnicity
of beadworkers and wearers in Ecuador has varied, but at present, bead
wearers in Ecuador, especially in the highlands, tend to be indigenous
women. Meisch summarizes her survey of such use as follows: "Beads
continue to be an important part of traditional dress for female *indige-
nas*, especially in the sierra. . . . Today the use of certain kinds and colours
of bead jewelry indicates indigenous ethnicity in general, but also the
wearer's community or subgroup, religion, wealth, and most of all, gender. Beads are such an essential part of indigenous female dress in the
Ecuadorian sierra that bead merchants and venders will have customers
for years to come" (1998b, 172).

The Saraguros were the first Ecuadorian highland group to incorporate multicolored glass beads into patterned, woven work. The local oral
version of the origin of this beadwork says that Saraguros who colonized
the rainforest in Zamora Province to the east of Saraguro encountered
Shuar people with beads. The women there began working with beads
and brought them back to the highlands, where woven necklaces became
increasingly popular throughout the middle and end of the twentieth century. This manner of beadwork remains a distinctive characteristic of the
Saraguros, with complex elaborations on the first simple *de colores* pattern
being invented by Saraguro women artisans every year. In her brief discussion of Saraguro bead weaving, Meisch describes *wallka tejidos* (a combination of Quichua [Q.] and Spanish, meaning "woven necklaces") as
"made from tiny, glass seed beads (Q. *mullus*) imported from Czechosla-
vakia, the United States, and possibly elsewhere. The beads are joined in
zig-zag rows (Q. *kingus*), and the number of rows and color combinations
indicate the wearer's community" (Meisch 1998b, 165). My research since
2005 suggests that while contemporary Saraguro women may verbally express the idea that the size and color choices indicate specific community
identity, the actual practice is that women artisans make and wear what-

ever color combinations and patterns strike their interest, and the size of necklaces is no longer limited to specific community identities.

However, there are some color combinations that contemporary Saraguro women seem to prefer, especially necklaces with a field of black and foreground patterns of blended shades of red, green, and blue. As a variety of high quality beads becomes available to the women (often brought back from Spain or the United States by family members working abroad), shimmering necklaces of precisely machined, single-color, metallic-finish beads are enjoying a popularity surge. While the oldest pattern of *de colores* is still seen as the most "proper" for traditional dress, experimentation is common, and new patterns, both for marketing and for personal use, emerge frequently and are shared liberally within and between communities.

TRADITION AND CREATIVITY

The experience of Ana Victoria, my primary beadwork teacher and friend in Saraguro, offers an interesting case of an individual working within her culture's traditions to express herself creatively. As such, she exemplifies emergent cultural creativity as described by Rosaldo, Lavie, and Narayan in the introduction of their edited volume on the study of creativity in anthropology: "Creativity . . . is always emergent. Members of a society's younger generation always select from, elaborate upon, and transform the traditions they inherit. The healthy perpetuation of cultural traditions requires invention as well as rote repetition" (1993, 5). The kind of blending of invention and repetition that Rosaldo, Lavie, and Narayan point to represents a logical extension of *la vida matizada*. Fluidity in creativity flows from the mix of daily needs, aesthetic pursuits, and the availability of materials for creating.

Andrea Heckman's remarkable book *Woven Stories: Andean Textiles and Rituals* highlights the creativity and innovation within tradition of many Andean artists. The book beautifully illustrates the culture, environment, and weaving motifs from the area around Ausangate Peak in highland central Peru. Heckman's weaver friends undermine her preconceptions about the relationship between tradition and change. Heckman says she anticipated that the "introduction of synthetic yarns and chemical dyes might signal the diminishing value of textile arts." But her weaver friends don't see this as a challenge to their own creative tradition. "We use synthetics because we like the bright colors. . . . The synthetic yarn is ugly. We respin all of it" (2003, 23).

The view of tradition not as some static condition when one kind of material, pattern, or ideal is valued but, rather, as a process of re-spinning the available materials to suit the needs and interests of the artist resonates with my understanding of women's art in Saraguro. What is traditional is the process embedded in the worldview of the artisans. The craftswomen of the cooperative do not see tradition as setting arbitrary limits on their creativity as artisans. The result is that they constantly experiment with new styles, seeking also to understand what aesthetics in other cultural settings will draw the attention of buyers of their art. Yet they maintain the social and creative cultural core of their activities by working together weekly, both to make aesthetic decisions and to distribute fairly the opportunities for work so that everybody benefits.

Ana Victoria does not promote herself as an artist superior to her friends and fellow artists in the community, but she fiercely identifies herself as a creative person whose very life has depended on her artistic commitments and practices.

Ana Victoria calls the story of her life, "my tragedy, my disaster" because of the early struggles she and her brothers experienced when their mother left the family. Her father died a few years later. The three children lived alone in the simple adobe house built by their father. She and Benigno still live in this house, with some additions and improvements, such as running water, that they have made since she and Benigno married more than fifteen years ago.

In the interview that follows, we discuss not only her life story but also the women's cooperative that she helped create. We also touch on her other community activities. She has been instrumental in the formation of a youth cultural group, Grupo Rumiñahui, which fields male and female teams in intercommunity sports (soccer and volleyball), participates in traditional dance competitions, and offers other activities for young people. Maximo, her brother, whose work life I discussed in chapter 2, was also important to the early formation of this cultural group, one spin-off of which was an Andean music ensemble, also named Rumiñahui, which toured in the United Stated in the 1990s and which opened the opportunity for Maximo to secure the legal permission to work in the United States.

The kind of emergent creativity demonstrated by Ana Victoria and Maximo as they considered the needs of their community for activities for themselves and other young people exemplifies the use of an anthropological consciousness to assess the cultural situation they live within. They performed a critical analysis of the community to understand that the young people needed this venue through which to value their culture.

They are not alone in this, of course, as the national conversation in Ecuador offers many examples of traditional ethnic life coming into dialogue with national goals and global realities. For example, the Rumiñahui dance group now has a Facebook page (www.facebook.com/grupo.rumi nahui?fref=ts) and competes in regional competitions with people from other ethnic groups. As is the case throughout the world in our global era, local life is created beyond simply the frame of the village.

The cultural creativity embodied in the work of the dance group and the craft cooperatives opens a means to participate in larger narratives of ethnicity and identity in a modern, pluralistic nation-state. Like individuals and communities throughout the globalizing world, Saraguros create culture day by day in imaginative acts seeking to create satisfactory lives. They are aware of the improvisational nature of this in a world where local, regional, national, and global forces all contribute to the on-the-ground realities of daily life. Ana Victoria exemplifies engaged creativity that feeds social as well as individual needs. For Ana Victoria, that feeding began as a literal act of survival.

ANA VICTORIA'S STORY

Ana Victoria: I started to make necklaces, when I was without my parents. My parents died. My mother abandoned me when I was six years old. She went to live . . . we didn't know where she went . . . but now she lives in Ambato [Ana Victoria's mother re-established contact with her children a few years ago]. And my father died from his grief at my mother leaving. He got sick, and he died. When he died I was ten years old. And we were alone. We didn't have anything to eat or anything. So, Maximo studied, and I started to work with a woman who lived a little ways down the hill whose name was Angelina. She taught me how to weave [beads]. I was her helper. And I spent four years beading with her. I only went to her house to work, and then came back here to our house to eat and do everything else. This very house! Only Maximo and I and a younger brother lived here. But he left, when he finished school, he went to the Coast, and he has lived on the Coast until now. His name is Marco.

Then, a few years passed and Maximo had the opportunity to go to the United States with a musical group. And I was left alone, alone, alone in the house. For three years. I say it was when I was fourteen until I was sixteen. When I was sixteen, I started being with Benigno. And when I was almost eighteen we got married. Then I was married, and I had fully learned how to bead — by this time I had continued to work with the beads. And back then I was able to sell a lot of beadwork because there were only a few people around who were beading. I was beading a lot, so I had money. Almost nobody was beading. There were very few beaders. This was more or less in 1995. More or less at this time nobody was beading. Now, there are a lot of beaders! Because now it is marketable. They can sell it. They can make money. So, this is the way that the beadwork became popular, so now the whole world beads! The *mestizas* [are beading] — everybody in the whole world is beading now!

David: But who is buying them?

Ana Victoria: The tourists!

David: But there are only a few tourists [here in Saraguro].

Ana Victoria: Many tourists! People go out to sell to them. There's a group organized to go sell in Loja, in Quito, in Guayaquil, in Vilcabamba — in all of the city markets. So the tourists go out to the markets and find beadwork on every side. So, for this reason, it is now very marketable to sell necklaces. And because so many people are beading beautiful things now, one can't sell one's work. So, for this reason I have to be very creative. When I come up with a new design, I make a dozen of them before I take them to the market. Because afterward, I'm not able to sell them. If I take a design [that is already common in the market, the storekeepers say,] "If you'll take $5 for it. [If I take new designs] nobody has copied them. Therefore, I need to take new designs to sell.

David: And so now there are lots of designs that are common. Which of these design are ones you made?

Ana Victoria: *Rosas, caracoles . . .*

David: Yes, *caracoles*, but, *caracoles* are originally from a guy in the United States!

Ana Victoria: Yes.

David: Then you copy, too!

Ana Victoria: I copy, yes, but I introduced it for the first time, after Linda [Belote] showed it to me. I made a dozen and then sold them.

David: So, you learned to bead because you needed to?

Ana Victoria: Because I needed to, yes.

David: It was your only life. For how many years — for four or six years?

Ana Victoria: For many years! I learned how to bead when I was eight, and now I am thirty-two. My life has been lived only in *artesanías*. Now, for example, I don't make only the necklaces. I make *polleras*, blouses, and the [bead] weavings, I sell them as a set. The *polleras*, the blouses, and the necklaces—this is the way I sell now—it's a three-piece suit. The same color—earrings, necklace, the blouse, and the *pollera*.

David: And how much does it cost for everything?

Ana Victoria: It depends on the necklace. The necklace might be worth twenty or thirty dollars, or it's possible to make a small one for ten dollars. It depends on the necklace. But the *pollera* and the blouse is worth thirty-five dollars. For only the *pollera* and blouse.

David: With beads, or with embroidery?

Ana Victoria: With a needle, and my hands! But the *pollera* I don't make by hand—I use a machine [currently an old treadle sewing machine adapted to use a motor, but she has ambitious plans for the future to purchase an expensive, computer-assisted embroidering machine].

David: Yes, but does the *pollera* come with beadwork [on the hem], or with embroidery?

Ana Victoria: Embroidery with thread. This is right now, the way of my work. This is what is now marketable, combined— the blouse the same color, the *pollera* the same color, the earrings the same color, and the necklace the same color.

David: And many women buy the whole set?

Ana Victoria: Yes. This is what's in style today—to wear a green blouse, green earrings, a green necklace, and a green *pollera*. Belts [*fajas*], too. I make belts with beads, too. I have one to show you. The belts sell for thirty dollars.

David: Las Calcutas, what importance do the Calcutas have for you?

Ana Victoria: For me? Perhaps it's a way to entertain myself first of all. But on the other hand, I like the organization.

David: Why?

Ana Victoria: Because it is also a way we women work together when we need to ask the mayor or any other institution for help; it's much easier. You can get support for an organization much easier than you can for one person. For this reason I like the organization. I always like to be part of an organization for any kind of thing in the community. In the end, for anything, it is very beautiful to be part of a group. On the other hand, doing something alone, without anybody, is really ugly. I always love for there to be a group to be with. For dancing there's one group of people—especially young people. For the young people's group we go out, we dance, we smile, we walk together, we do things that makes us smile and laugh. And for the women's group, it's another group of people who like to do things together. So, I like to organize things all the time. I like to get involved.

David: So, the idea of community is very important for you?

Ana Victoria: I like to go to [community] meetings, to be involved in the community. Last year I was the secretary of the community. And it was very complicated for me. It was very hard. I'd have to go to Saraguro and arrive there by seven in the evening, and there might be no dinner here because I like to be on time. For anything, if someone says [be there] at three, I am there five minutes before, because I like to be punctual, so that yes, I am there on time. For example, the women's cooperative is supposed to meet at 2:30 in the afternoon. We should all be there by then. If you get there at three, then you have to pay twenty-five cents. If anybody comes at three, they pay twenty-five cents for being late. So we have lots of money—because the whole world is always late! But this is one way to make sure we all arrive at the same time. This is one of the forms of our organization of women, we say, "If you don't arrive on time, you don't work equally with all of us. If you don't arrive until three, you haven't done the same amount of work as the others. If you don't arrive until three, you have to pay the twenty-five cents for the work that others have made." It's an extra protection to make sure everybody arrives on time.

David: And how many women are in Las Calcutas?

Ana Victoria: Eighteen.

David: And everybody comes every time or no?

Ana Victoria: Yes. Almost all every time. One time we might be fifteen, thirteen, twelve. We can sometimes miss with permission. Someone sometimes says, "This time I can't come, but I worked on something on an earlier day." But mostly we all meet on the same day. For example, if I can't go on a certain Tuesday, I'll make a weaving [necklace] in my house. If I have to do some other work on a Tuesday I'll make something to contribute to the group. To make everything fair, I'll make something at home. It's a form to equalize the work that we do.

David: And the money you make together, you own together, right?

Ana Victoria: Yes, right now we have money—capital—when we make beads and sell them, we deposit the money in an account. This money is considered sacred. We don't take it out. Because we want to have a large capital base to make a big project. Our thought right now is to build a house [not a residence, but a building to serve as a women's community center]. So we have worked really hard to get together the money to buy the property.

David: How much do you need to build the center?

Ana Victoria: Oh, a lot! The piece of land alone cost us eight thousand dollars.

David: Without a building?

Ana Victoria: Yes. Without a building. And we need to buy materials for construction. We need to pay for construction. We need to hire a contractor. We think we might hire this guy [gesturing to Benigno, her husband], but he comes very expensive, so maybe we won't be able to do the construction! [Everybody laughs.]

David: Good work isn't cheap!

Ana Victoria: Yes. He asks for a lot, so maybe we won't be able to build.

Benigno: No, what has happened is that two years have gone by without action, so maybe you don't value my work!

Ana Victoria: You can't eat in the house! [She laughs.]

Benigno: They want to say that when they sell their beads, then they want to pay me. What am I supposed to eat right now?

David: And the other women have the same idea, to make a house [for a community center]?

Ana Victoria: You mean other groups of women in other communities? I don't know. Their better thoughts might be different. But our idea is to have a house for our group of women to use. And perhaps some space for our youth group to use. Because the youth group neither has a place. This is the aim of our work, and the aspiration that we desire.

David: And you use the money you make together only in this manner?

Ana Victoria: Every year we get a small gift.

David: Oh?

Ana Victoria: For the work that we make; this is a gift for each person. This past year we got about a hundred dollars [worth of items such as food, kitchen items, and other small, useful things].

David: Every woman?

Ana Victoria: Every woman. Our organization is always open. We work transparently with every woman. Up to this time, we've not had one problem—with money, not one problem. Everybody knows how much money we have. Everybody knows what we are going to do with the money. Everybody knows . . . and all the women together say, "This is something we are going to do, and this we are not." We meet all together. We work all together, and so, this is our money. When everybody has seen the money we have, then we deposit it. We all know how much money we have for deposit. We meet anew and work together some more on necklaces, take them to the market, or sometimes Silvia [Rosa's daughter, who lives and works in the United States] carries our necklaces to the States. And we send the necklaces to the United States, and she says, "Here is the money for the necklaces you sent to the States, here is the money." And we deposit. Here are the books, where we keep track of the capital we have. And everybody knows. Everybody says this is the amount we have. And so, for this amount of work for this month, we see how much we make. The work is sociable. One day, for example, someone might say, "Today I don't have the urge to work. Today I'm going to make food [for everyone]." And we say, "Yes, you go cook, and we will work." We all contribute the same to the organization. We don't say, "I'll put ten cents, you put twenty cents, fifty cents." We keep things united and even in anything we do. Sometimes nobody weaves [works on necklaces]. We go . . . for example, on a *minga* [work party], that one of our friends [needs]. For example, "I need the help of all of the women of la Calcutas." And everyone comes to my place and works, and that's what we do on some Tuesdays.

David: For example, what kind of work?

Ana Victoria: For example, here in recent months the corn has become ripe . . . if I need many people to help harvest the corn, for one. Or another thing, Señora Alejita made a *minga* about a month ago, for us to help bring stones from the river to make a wall outside the house. All the women were working. We always work cooperatively. All together. If you go, I do, too. All go. And we do the work. And it's good. Beautiful. Never do we have a problem, for example, over money. No. Neither do we have any grudges. Politically we have a few grudges, because some women are for other parties and others are for another party. So we have a little political clash. Politically we have some grudges. But they pass. The political [season] finishes, and the problems end.

Interlude 3

LOS CARACOLES: TRAVELS
AND TRANSFORMATIONS
OF AESTHETIC IDEAS

*Invention takes place within a field of culturally available possibilities,
rather than being without precedent. It is as much a process of selection
and recombination as one of thinking anew. Creativity emerges from
past traditions and moves beyond them; the creative persona reshapes
traditional forms. The circumstances of creativity admit to contact,
borrowing, and conflict. Regarded as a field of creativity, the zones
of interaction among and within cultures more nearly resemble the
overlapping strands of a rope than separate beads on a string.*

RENATO ROSALDO, SMADAR LAVIE, AND KIRIN NARAYAN,
INTRODUCTION TO *CREATIVITY/ANTHROPOLOGY* (LAVIE,
NARAYAN, AND ROSALDO 1993)

*What is the charm of necklaces? Why would anyone put something
extra around her neck and then invest it with special significance?
A necklace doesn't afford warmth in cold weather, like a scarf, or
protection in combat, like chain mail; it only decorates. We might say it
borrows meaning from what it surrounds and sets off: the head with its
supremely important material contents, and the face, that register of
the soul. . . . When people are intensely concerned with something that
is obviously impractical, anthropologists take note, for lovely useless
things often express archaic structures in the human soul.*

EMILY R. GROSHOLZ, "ON NECKLACES" (2007)

Las Mujeres de Teresa de Calcuta of Tuncarta display some of their necklaces as they prepare to send them to the Santa Fe International Folk Art Market in 2010. The cooperative plans to build a women's cultural center with future earnings.

Petrona, Benigno's mother, on her way to town, wearing the de colores *pattern, universally considered the "most traditional" by the women, along with strands of metallic, gold-finished beads.*

*I*N 2003 THE ANTHROPOLO-gist Linda Belote (2003) introduced readers of the U.S.-based craft magazine *Bead and Button* to the distinctive necklaces made and worn by the women of Saraguro. These necklaces have been part of the traditional dress of the Saraguros since about the 1950s. As their work has been increasingly appreciated by nonindigenous Ecuadorians and people from other countries, the artists of the community have experimented with new designs to expand their repertoire. It is still possible to see the basic *de colores* pattern, but as with any traditional art, changing tastes and styles, a desire for new and different patterns, and access to more colors and better quality beads has led to an explosion of creativity.

My beading teacher, Ana Victoria, like others in her community, is an innovative bead artist and constantly creates new designs for necklaces. When I visited her in July 2009, she was working on a new model patterned after the large june bugs common in Saraguro. She showed me a prototype of the piece, which was a fairly radical departure from the patterns commonly made. It was directly representational and made with very loose, open netting. The june bugs stretched across the whole piece and were portrayed in red on a black background. She was not satisfied with the results and said she would refine the design before producing a dozen or more of them to be sold. Saraguro bead artists are effective copiers, and when a new pattern hits the market, they quickly examine and reproduce

Ana Victoria modeling a variation of an elegante *(elegant) necklace she had just designed.* Elegantes *are usually made to be sold rather than worn by Saraguro women themselves.*

This model was in widespread production beginning about 2008. The website www.saraguro.org /beadwork.htm, created and maintained by Linda and Jim Belote, offers numerous examples of styles from the 1960s to the present.

Aleja Medina González, with her daughter Paulina, invented this pattern, called fresas *(strawberries), after studying photos in an art book Linda Belote brought to the women.*

it, so the "fresh" shelf life of a new pattern is brief. Ana Victoria always makes at least a dozen of any new pattern so that she can be ahead of the curve to effectively sell her work before mimicry disrupts her brief monopoly on the new patterns she creates. The styles preferred by the women depend on the availability and colors of quality beads and on their assessment, in consultation with advisors such as Linda Belote and the bead artist Ann Severine, of what will sell, especially in the United States.

Laughter, joking, and high spirits often fill the meetings of the cooperative.

Rosa Medina Sarango beading on the patio of her home. When the members of the cooperative are unable to attend meetings, they work on their own time on pieces for the group.

In Tuncarta, the women of La Cooperativa Teresa de Calcuta meet every Tuesday afternoon to work on collective pieces to be sold to benefit the cooperative. All of the necklaces made during this work time belong to the cooperative, which uses the proceeds from sales to purchase materials for further work. The cooperative also provides micro loans to members when needed and contributes to community projects and festivals.

"I've noticed you don't usually use white as the basis for your patterns—why is this?" I asked as they worked during a meeting. Everyone paused before one woman spoke up and turned my question into an opportunity for teasing.

"We use black because we're black! If white people did this kind of work, they're the ones who should use white as the base!"

Laughter and more jokes followed.

"We use black because it combines well with any color and matches our clothes," one woman concluded and others nodded and agreed.

When I arrived one day to inter-

Mariana Lozano in 2009 working on a necklace commissioned by a nonbeading Saraguro woman who lives in the Amazon.

view Mariana Lozano, we sat on her porch while she worked and we talked. The solid-color gold necklace she was working on was commissioned by a Saraguro woman who lived in the Amazon basin to the east of the highlands. The woman from the Amazon basin did not do beadwork herself, something that Mariana said is not unusual for women who have left the highlands. Mariana had completed many commissioned necklaces for such women, who purchased the beads and paid her a small fee to make the necklaces. The solid-color style has become popular as people who

travel abroad have returned with these beads, which have not been locally available.

Mariana has a photo of her younger self in a photo album that was taken by a visiting anthropologist in the 1980s. She allowed me to take photos of this old photograph and another of her mother

Mariana Lozano in the 1980s; this photo was taken by a visiting anthropologist. Courtesy of Mariana Lozano.

In 2009 Mariana allowed me to copy this photo of her family from the 1970s. It shows Mariana and her siblings with her mother and father nearly forty years ago. Courtesy of Mariana Lozano.

Ana Victoria considers how best to display her cooperative's beadwork as she sets up for the 2010 Santa Fe International Folk Art Market.

The anthropologist Linda Belote and Ana Victoria Sarango review the inventory list at the 2010 Santa Fe International Folk Art Market.

Ana Victoria visits with an artist/vendor from China at the 2010 Santa Fe Market.

and father from nearly forty years earlier. She pointed with pride to the things in the photo that were her mother's handiworks — including several *de colores* necklaces that are much larger than the models I see women wearing now. Other handmade items included embroidered blouses, woven wool blankets, belts, and ponchos. In the photo, her mother spins with a horizontal spindle. The elder brother holds the family puppy so that it is looking at the camera. Everybody except the mother looks at the camera. Mariana's mother focuses on her handwork, as if she could not take time away from this basic task even to pose for a moment.

Mariana said the full name of the oldest pattern is *de colores de Jivaro*, so named because it was the Jivaro people (now called the Shuar) of the Amazon who first traded beads with the Saraguros. It is significant that even the oldest, most traditional pattern of bead weaving acknowledges in its name that the process of creativity involves cross-cultural contact and aesthetic borrowing.

Another interesting case of aesthetic borrowing and development emerged from the women's participation in the Santa Fe International Folk Art Market.

The market provides both a sales venue and training for the artists in pricing, display, and accessing international clientele. The story of the development and acceptance of a new pattern for necklaces highlights the ways that transnational contact can shape what are considered traditional art forms. In 2006 a U.S. bead artist named Ross Nance approached the booth where Linda Belote and Ann Severine assisted a Saraguro woman as she was selling for her cooperative. He had a necklace he had been making that he wanted to share. Using patterns available on the Internet, he had been experimenting with the Saraguro technique of necklace making to create a running pattern across the piece. The pattern resembled a running motif found in various Greek and Roman artworks—for example, in mosaics. Mr. Nance said that looking at Incan textile patterns inspired his design.

Linda photographed Ross Nance's model and carried the photos with her to Saraguro when she next visited. She gave each of the women's cooperatives a copy of the new design. She introduced the pattern to Saraguro beaders as *Incaiko*, or "Incan." Beaders in several communities, including Ana Victoria in Tuncarta, worked out how the pattern was made, adapted the color choices to Saraguro preferences, and began making it to wear and to sell. The women of Las Calcutas Cooperative have taken to calling the piece *caracoles*, "snail shells," for its spiraling aspect. Mr. Nance's version offered many colors not in the usual palette of Saraguro artists. When I asked Ana Victoria about the original, she explained that she thought the pattern was beautiful but that the color combinations were not *matizado*, and I again realized the importance

Luz Magdalena Macas Minga wearing the caracoles *pattern necklace she made for herself.*

of this concept to her aesthetic sense. The Saraguro variations on the pattern tend to have a black background, with the pattern worked in *matizado* blends of blue, red, green, or purple.

It is now possible to find the *caracoles* pattern in at least half a dozen shops and stands in Saraguro and beyond. At the Sunday market, I have seen many women

Ana Victoria with Benigno's sister, Nila, and my daughter, at the beading table. It is not unusual for one or more people are learning beading techniques to join Ana Victoria each d the table on the porch to work.

wearing very large versions of the necklace, with the *caracoles* pattern repeated three times around the piece. Once when Carmen, a cousin to Ana Victoria, sat working on such a piece at Ana Victoria's beading table, I explained to Carmen that this pattern came from a male beadworker in the United States. She expressed surprise. When I asked her why she was making it, she said, "Because it's beautiful." I told her I thought it was adapted from a Greek pattern; she just shrugged and kept on beading.

The Saraguro adaptation has been picked up and transformed again by at least one nonindigenous Ecuadorian bead artist as well. In Cuenca, I encountered a bead artist named Pedro. He works as a dentist, but on Sundays he spreads a cloth on the ground in the central square known as Parque Calderón, and he sells the beadwork he has made. His work includes large loomed bracelets, bags, and other pieces, as well as Saraguro-style necklaces. The day I saw him, he prominently displayed a *caracoles* design in a stunning color combination of matte black and shiny gold beads. It was the centerpiece of his collection.

Pedro commented that Saraguro artists use colors that don't always appeal to nonindigenous buyers and that the styles are always the same. Pedro's comments are not accurate, as Linda

Belote's extensive collection of Saraguro pieces dating back to the 1960s suggests that there have always been a lot of creative exploration of patterns and colors (for examples, see the gallery of *collares* at www.saraguro.org/beadwork.htm). Pedro attributed this perceived sameness to aesthetics, which is partially true—the women of Saraguro do seem to prefer certain *matizada* color combinations—but it is also an issue of access and expense. Pedro locates diverse beads of high quality to use in his work, and he can afford them.

Bead choice is shaped in all three cases—the U.S. bead artist, the Saraguro artists, and the nonindigenous artist—by larger spheres of aesthetic and practical realities that determine the possibilities for what is "traditional folk art" and what might be considered "individual expressive art."

All the artists at the Santa Fe Market identify a selected piece that they feel represents their best work. This piece, chosen by Ana Victoria, is labeled "Artist's Choice" and displayed prominently for sale.

CHAPTER FIVE

Sweet Water and Exotic Fish

ECOLOGICAL IMAGINATIONS IN A
WORLD OF TRAVELING CREATURES

*Many complain that the words of the wise are always merely parables
and of no use in daily life, which is the only life we have. When the sage
says: "Go over," he does not mean that we should cross to some actual
place, which we could do anyhow if the labor were worth it; he means
some fabulous yonder, something unknown to us, something too that he
cannot designate more precisely, and therefore cannot help us here in
the very least. All these parables really set out merely to say that the
incomprehensible is incomprehensible, and we know that already. But the
cares with which we have to struggle every day: that is a different matter.*

*Concerning this a man once said: Why such reluctance? If you only
followed the parables, you yourselves would become parables and, with
that, rid of all your daily cares.*

Another said: I bet that is also a parable.

The first said: You have won.

The second said: But unfortunately only in parable.

The first said: No, in reality: in parable you have lost.

FRANZ KAFKA, "ON PARABLES" (1971, 457)

*Esto debe ser más que un texto, la voz de la Pachamama que convoca a
mantener, crear y recrear los saberes en las communidades. Le invitamos a
no perder la oportunidad de re-encontrar con la vida misma. [This should
be more than a text, the voice of Pachamama (Mother Earth) continues
to call, creates and recreates knowledge in our communities. We invite you
not to lose the opportunity to re-find life itself.]*

ANGEL GUALÁN AND PEDRO POMA, *MITOS, CUENTOS Y
LEYENDAS DEL PUEBLO SARAGURO* (2006, 9)

When Benigno begins a tale, he first makes sure to say whether it is a story (*cuento*) or it is both a story and a legend (*leyenda*). The distinction is important to him. If the events of the tale involve only animals, it is a *cuento*; if humans are the major characters, the tale is a *leyenda*. Benigno is a patient storyteller. He pauses to rethink how to relate the events of the stories whenever I am unsure about his meaning. We spend many nights trading funny *cuentos* about how Rabbit tricks Fox and Bear.

One night, however, we moved out of the times when animals spoke to one another and into the time when humans became primary actors on the scene. In this world, the rules changed, and the consequences of human actions could be severe. In the animal-based world of the *cuentos*, cleverness is its own reward, and manipulating other creatures is seen as a source of humor. In the *leyendas*, when humans treat the creatures or resources of the world badly or take them for granted, the potential for reprisal from natural forces and human loss are the order of the day. Stories that Benigno identifies as legends usually begin and end with some version of a statement of truthfulness, "It's a story, but it's true." The purpose of this phrasing is to emphasize that this *leyenda*, unlike the *cuentos*, conveys significant information about moral responsibilities and realities. The legends encode lessons showing how to live *la vida matizada* properly. Benigno and my other friends in Tuncarta relish telling tales about mysterious places. Saraguro people have published several collections of local legends and tales, including the one cited in the epigraph to this chapter, and they clearly desire to make them relevant to present lives.

Benigno tells of human activities in the landscape that also productively rub against the kinds of science and culture stories I hear in the Great Lakes region while working as a teacher, researcher, and environmental writer and activist. The narrative shape of two of the *leyendas* Benigno told about human activity around Andean highland lakes resonates strongly with the stories told by scientists about the invasion of exotic species in the Great Lakes of the United States. Control of natural resources in the Saraguro area, as in the United States, struggles to keep pace with the changing realities of a growing local population as well as with increasing globalization of the economic and social realities of the place. This has become an arena for the kinds of frictions I have been discussing throughout this book. The two *leyendas* and the science story re-told in this chapter revolve around traveling animals as the source of friction in a world where humans, wealth, and all kinds of natural resources move across great distances.

Each story offers culturally distinctive answers to the question of how humans fit within and manipulate ecological processes. The kind of imagination embodied in Benigno's stories fits closely with the idea of *la vida matizada*—that is, accepting that humans fit within ecological processes is part of the blended daily life that my Saraguro friends seek to live.

Juxtaposing Benigno's *leyendas* with a scientific story of the invasion of sea lampreys in the Great Lakes reveals intriguing similarities and differences in the cultural underpinnings of an indigenous Andean storytelling tradition and scientific narratives of resource management. Indeed, the juxtaposition of these two ways of thinking about the world creates a fruitful reminder that science, like oral storytelling, is fundamentally a way of *imagining* the relationships between different parts of the natural and social world. Both Benigno's stories and the scientific tale reflect on ecological processes, especially related to a specific kind of disturbance—the presence of an exotic, introduced species. The ways that people interpret the presence of an exotic species in each context suggest deeply rooted cultural ideas about the human place within the environment.

By bringing these disparate storytelling traditions together, I explore how ecological imaginations are inevitably inflected by cultural ideas and how such inflections can create limits to understanding and responding to anthropogenic ecological change. I also use the idea of parables as parabolic cultural mirrors to emphasize the nature of the ethnographic encounter as it creates an anthropological consciousness that straddles social worlds to create a productive space for reflecting on ways in which the lives of humans blend with the ecological worlds we inhabit.

PEOPLE TRAVELING OVER MOUNTAINS

Since the early 1900s, the Yacuambí Valley, located about forty kilometers to the east of Saraguro on the Amazonian side of the Continental Divide, has become an expansion site for a growing Saraguro population. The Saraguros use this area to raise cattle. Many Saraguro families have established holdings in the Yacuambí Valley while maintaining a residence in the more traditional highland areas around Saraguro. Foot travel over the Continental Divide became common in the middle of the twentieth century, and under ideal circumstances Saraguros can make the one-way trip in a single day of rapid walking. However, the journey can become dangerous during periods of cold, wet, or windy weather. People traveling to and from the Oriente (the commonly used Ecuadorian name for the Amazon Basin, located in the eastern portion of the country) have sometimes been caught in such weather while crossing the high pass and plains. Jim Belote (1984, 222), in the prologue to the section of his dissertation describing life for the Saraguros in the valley, quotes the Franciscan padre of Yacuambí, who called the trip from Saraguro to Yacuambí "the descent into Hell." The journey drains bodily resources. Some Saraguros have died from hypothermia when caught in bad weather in the crossing.

Benigno is the oldest of nine children, but he is the only offspring of his biological father and his biological mother, Petrona. When Petrona was pregnant with Benigno, her husband attempted to make the trip back from the Oriente to Tuncarta with two cows. A squall struck in the crossing, and he died from exposure. He was discovered the following day by other travelers who found the cattle alive and returned to Tuncarta with the body and the animals. The death of his father left an indelible mark on Benigno. Ana Victoria calls him *el unico*, the unique one, and he seems to be a different sort of person from his younger brothers and sisters. He is something of an elder figure to them, and he is also someone intellectually engaged by the contrasts between traditional and modern life. Some of this difference can be attributed to the impact of his paternal grandfather on Benigno. Benigno became both an economic heir and, as significantly, a cultural heir to his paternal grandfather, who stepped in as a protector and influence after Benigno's father died.

Benigno took me to the *finca*, or small farm, he inherited from his grandfather. He clearly reveres both the land he now owns and the memories and stories he harbors of his grandfather. He showed me the remains of the small adobe house on the hillside where his grandfather lived and told me that he plans to rebuild the structure. Throughout my stays with Benigno, he shares his cultural and agricultural knowledge, as well as stories that he often says he learned from his grandfather, such as the two *leyendas* that follow. Both stories constitute part of the legacy Benigno's grandfather left him.

THE LEGENDS

Leyenda 1: *The Sweetening of Siri Wiña*

There's a place in the *cerro*, the upland region, above here. It is called Fier Urco, and it's a beautiful place. This is a story, but it's the truth. One lake there is called Siri Wiña. One day two men were coming home carrying a pile of *caña* [sugarcane] between them. They were planning to make *miel de caña* [literally, "honey of the cane" — a liquid sweetener] from the cane. They were tired and hungry, so they set the pile down beside the lake and ate their lunch and rested a while. While they rested, a light rain fell on them and the pile of cane.

After a while the two men were ready to go on, so they tried to lift the pile of cane, but the rain had accumulated inside the pile, making it heavier than before. The men decided to try to lighten the load by lifting one end of the pile higher than the other to drain the water off into the lake and lighten the load. But when they did so, the pile slipped into the lake, floated out into the middle of the lagoon, and sank to the bottom. The men tried to make a small boat out of nearby materials so they could float over the sunken pile and try to retrieve it. They tried several times to raise the cane, but because the water was deep and the cane was now heavily saturated with water, they couldn't.

The men were furious—they had hauled that pile a long, long way, and they really wanted to make *miel de caña* with it for their families, so they ran back to their community and organized a work party. They returned to the lake with their families and began to dig a canal to drain the lake and reveal the pile beneath the water.

But just as the water began to run into the canal and started to drain the lake, it began to rain and thunder, and huge bolts of lightning filled the sky and struck close to the people. They became worried. Then, from someplace they could not see, they heard loud, angry sounds of many animals—horses, bulls, sheep, goats—ugly, ugly sounds. They became terrified, and all the people ran away, abandoning the canal, which soon stopped carrying water away from the lake. They never finished their work, and the pile of cane remained at the bottom of the lake. It can't be seen anymore, but the water of that lake is sweet and good for trout. It's a story, but it's the truth.

Leyenda 2: *The Boy Who Threw Stones at Ducks*

Another story—it's true—is about a boy who lived near Pila Cocha, another lake in Fier Urco, in a community called Sunin. Every day the boy and a friend had the job of taking the community's cows up to the *cerro* for pasture. Every day, as they led the animals up to the grazing grounds, they passed very close to Pila Cocha. One day, as they were returning from the *cerro*, they saw large flocks of ducks floating on the waters of the lagoon. The boy sent his friend on with the cows—he wanted to see whether he could kill some ducks by throwing stones at them. He picked up a rock and flung it at a nearby duck—he missed, but the rock startled a bunch of them, and they took off in a great flapping of wings and much disturbance of the water.

The boy laughed. He thought this was one of the funniest things he had ever seen, so he went all around the lagoon throwing rocks at clusters of ducks simply to harass them and watch them fly away.

Suddenly it began to rain very fiercely. The air became so thick with cold water that the boy could not see in front of him. He hunkered down and shivered in the rain as he got drenched and became very cold. Soon he realized that if he didn't get to some shelter he would likely die of the cold, so he stumbled along the path the cows had worn into the ground and eventually made his way back to Sunin, where his family took him in, half frozen and unable to move his arms. They put him beside a fire and took care of him.

It rained for days, huge sheets of water, enough to make the lake flood over the fields and surrounding pastures. When the rain stopped and the water receded, the people of Sunin found that immense trout had come out of the lake and eaten all of the corn and grass from the fields and pastures. It's a story, but it's the truth.

DRAWING OUT THE ECOLOGICAL IMAGINATION IN THE LEGENDS

By "ecological imagination," I mean imagination about the ecological processes in the midst of which cultures live, but also imagination as shaped by environment. We imagine our world in particular ways because of the particular ecological locations and experiences within which we dwell. For example, I live in a society that has increasingly cushioned people from the ecological realities surrounding us. When my consciousness encounters a dilemma related to the environment that I live within, my ecological imagination tends to turn to abstractions and expediencies. In other words, if you live in a world where the greatest direct threat you experience from the ecological realities that surround you is an increased heating bill during a particularly cold winter, how you imagine ecological processes is likely to be cast in the instrumental language of science and its applied adjunct, economics.

In a cultural context such as that of Saraguro, where the experience of ecological realities is more direct, how you imagine ecological processes will likely be more personalized and, I argue, more *matizada*, or blended, with your sense of your place in the world. In other words, if you live in a world where your father or son can be killed by the weather, you are much more likely to cast your understanding of something like the presence of nonnative fish in the particularized and personalized terms offered by *leyendas*. The *leyendas* construct ecological realities not as only good or bad but rather as variable and ambiguous, indeed, as a negotiated *matizada* blending of human and nonhuman worlds.

The two stories Benigno told suggest cultural readings regarding how one imagines the environmental realities of a place, as well as the possible repercussions of disrupting the ecological cycles of that place. These stories meditate on the ways that changing the natural order of things can draw reprisals from the natural world. At least superficially they say that when people do something to disturb the ecological patterns of a place—such as drain a lake or gratuitously harass animals—the entire community pays a price (threatening sounds, excessive rain, and destructive consumption of pasture grasses). The simple message here is "Don't carelessly mess with the forces of nature."

However, both stories also contain another kind of thinking about ecological processes, especially relating to a specific kind of disturbance—the presence of an exotic, traveling species, the trout. At this level of environmental imagining, the relationship between disrupting the environment and repercussions to human cultures grows more complicated, indicating an ambivalent attitude to the question of how humans fit within and manipulate ecological processes. Trout, an exotic species that has been deliberately cultivated in Saraguro streams and lakes, are treasured as a food and economic resource. They also become, in these stories and in intercommunity relations, sources of new environmental and social tensions. As nonnative, they become focal points for cultural attention in a changing world, a process suggested by Paul Shepard in his book, *The Others: How Animals Made Us Human*:

> Another source of fringe animals is those not native to "this" place.
> ... Both types of marginal forms—those which are familiar, but do
> not fit our definitions, and those which we may encounter as trav-
> elers—disturb the primal model of an orderly world, producing
> taxonomic crisis and cognitive dissonance. Being paradoxical or
> "out of place" means discord, a wrenching of the cosmos, as when
> a wolf pack invades the village or a bear wanders into the city. This

perplexity seems to call for an explanation, for meaning that can be symbolically interpreted and spiritually significant. . . . If we repress these organisms, like all repressed material they can erupt into our dreams or stir our unconscious life in powerful ways. Official society tends to prohibit or regulate their expression. Yet they are precious; their very ambiguity seems to sharpen other definitions. (1996, 60–61)

Benigno's *leyendas* imply that exotic trout have become one focal point for cultural imaginings in terms of relations to the natural environment. In the imagination that underpins these two stories, the ambiguity of the trout as part of the local environment can be seen first in the fact that the waters of the region need to be prepared to host the nonnative trout, that is, Siri Wiña must be "sweetened" to make an ideal habitat for this new creature. And in the second story, the trout play the role of natural reprisal for inappropriate environmental behavior—the new species reverses its role from being a food source to being a consumer of food resources on which the community depends.

These stories suggest that in terms of relations between individuals and communities in the region, trout have come to play a significant yet ambiguous role. That ambiguity, as suggested by Shepard, serves as a point of cultural reflection that brings to light social tensions. By being out of place, trout provide a focal point for thinking about social change and for clarifying how the social landscape is contested. Some additional ethnographic context for the stories helps to develop this idea.

There have been tensions, especially between local indigenous communities, over who has rights of access to local resources. In the 1930s and 1940s, the governments of several Andean nations issued a request for reports of any native fish in highland lakes or streams that might offer viable stock for a sport fishing industry. Given the geological youth of the Andean range (65 million years or less), and hence the relatively short evolutionary time span, the call yielded no native fish of any size. Commercial-size fish simply have not had time to evolve in the cold waters of the highlands (Jim Belote, personal communication, January 8, 2006).

Following this failed attempt to identify an indigenous game fish, various governments (both national and local) as well as community groups began introducing nonnative trout species to highland streams and lakes. According to Jim Belote (personal communication, January 8, 2006), a small group of avid indigenous fishermen from Saraguro hauled seventy-pound bags filled with water and fingerlings over a mountain trail to highland lakes that are several hours' walk from the nearest road. The cold, clear waters of these streams and lakes offer an ideal habitat for certain types of fish, and the result has been the establishment of viable, reproducing populations of trout in many Ecuadorian waters, including the streams and lakes in the Saraguro region. To the delight of many Saraguro anglers and many other Ecuadorians (and a few outsider anthropologists), trout fishing in the Andes has become a reality over the last fifty years. Some enterprising Ecuadorians have capitalized on interest in trout by creating trout parks where people can use baited hooks to pluck farmed trout from holding tanks.

Some people in Saraguro hope to expand this resource as a tourist draw, but no significant economic development in the Saraguro area has yet come of this. However, my fieldwork and the stories I am discussing here indicate that significant social tensions accompany this boon to anglers. I have traveled several times with Benigno to fish in the Río Hierba Buena and to visit a locally significant waterfall known as Virgen Caca or Virgen Peña. The plunge pool at the base of the waterfall is a good location for trout fishing, and Benigno catches several from this place each time we visit. To reach the plunge pool we pass through the communities of Tambopamba and Oñacapac, the latter of which is located closest to the falls and by tradition is considered the *dueño*, or "owner," of the falls and of the small shrine to the Virgin that is located there. The concept of ownership, especially of natural resources, is complex in Saraguro, which, like many other Andean communities, has a strong tradition of reciprocity. It appears that such "ownership" is currently being renegotiated in the dynamic context of community social relations, raising questions of how best to manage a commons-based resource such as a river.

Benigno explained that his own community, Tuncarta, received a grant from a local foundation to which the community added donated labor to stock the river with two thousand trout fingerlings. He said that he has had encounters with Oñacapans who told him that he should not be fishing at the waterfall because it is located within the area of Oñacapac. Despite these warnings, Benigno and other Tuncartans believe they have a legitimate right to fish the length of the river because of their stocking work, which benefits everyone in the watershed.

During one visit with me to the waterfall, Benigno was accosted by an Oñacapan and told not to fish there. Another time, when I decided to walk back from the falls while Benigno remained behind to fish, a man from Oñacapac, who was clearly drunk, waited to intercept me and a group of three students at the top of a hill. He berated us for visiting "La Virgen" and told us that the location belonged to his community and that we gringos were not welcome there. During this confrontation, he asserted several times that the fish there belong to his community.

Benigno reports that Oñacapac has instituted what is locally an unusual method for managing a natural resource—if a person wishes to fish above the falls, he or she must pay five dollars (equivalent to half a day's wages for many people in Saraguro) for an eight-hour "permit." Although this might be seen as an ecological decision to reduce pressure on the fishery or an economic strategy to benefit the community, the fact is that local people from outside Oñacapac do not see the benefit of paying such an exorbitant fee for access when you could come away with no fish. In essence, the permission fee is an exclusionary strategy to keep local people from outside the community of Oñacapac from fishing the upper reaches of the river. The ambiguous, out-of-place exotic trout serve to sharpen social definitions and frictions between communities.

Benigno and Ana Victoria told a story that highlights local tensions over the control of natural resources. An artesian well bubbles up within the region claimed by Oñacapans. The people of Tuncarta wanted to access some of the well's output to provide water for the community. They hoped to create a covered canal or pipe to bring the water down the valley. Ana Victoria said Tuncarta went to the national government and established a legal claim to the water in the early 1980s, but a few years later the Oñacapans did the same, and the latter have been able to assert their rights over the Tuncartans, despite the earlier claim. Ana Victoria said the rumor is that Oñacapan community leaders thought they would be able to negotiate a deal with Tessalia, a corporation that sells bottled water in Ecuador, to put in a bottling plant. The deal never materialized, and now the Oñacapans have a well that they cannot afford to fully develop, and in the meantime, the people farther down the valley have been forced to find other sources of drinking water.

PARABLES AS PARABOLIC MIRRORS: ETHNOGRAPHIC ENCOUNTERS AS CULTURAL REFLECTORS

At this point, I want to move from thinking about these legends in an isolated ethnographic context to thinking about how juxtaposing these stories with a parable from my "own" culture can illuminate cultural inflections of environmental imaginaries. Using Shepard's (1996, 90–98) work on the "ecology of narration," I posit that, although a story such as the invasion of sea lamprey in the Great Lakes superficially has the same message as Benigno's stories, the imagination that underlies how the sea lamprey story gets told differs greatly from that of the stories of sweetening the waters of Siri Wiña or throwing stones at ducks. Where Benigno structures his stories largely with social concerns with immediate connections to people's lives, the scientific parable told about the sea lamprey invasion largely removes human agency from causes. The story of lamprey in the Great Lakes serves primarily, if unintentionally, to legitimize scientific agency in the matter of solutions: that is, to encourage a view of scientific wildlife management as a Promethean effort to solve the problem of the sea lamprey.

In making this juxtaposition, I see value in treating culturally shaped stories as parabolic mirrors; that is, by closely considering parables out of the imagination of a Saraguro storyteller, I can critically focus attention on my own culture's ecological imagination. Engaging with Benigno's *matizada*-inflected imagination has shifted my ideas about my home landscape. This juxtaposition does not have the primary goal of illuminating a distant, exotic culture; rather, it allows me to use cross-cultural juxtaposition as a tool for defamiliarizing the kind of stories told here at "home." In so doing, I am responding to the challenge presented by anthropologists such as Margaret Mead and others to bring anthropological insights back home. Marcus and Fischer (1986) argue for this approach when they write in favor of a repatriated form of anthropology that does not settle for merely traveling to and describing "peripheries." They write: "The challenge of serious cultural criticism is to bring the insights gained on the periphery back to the center to raise havoc with our settled ways of thinking and conceptualizing" (1986, 138).

I have participated in multiple types of environmental activism in the United States for more than a decade and have become somewhat anesthetized to the cultural norms that underlie the stories that environmentalists tell about their work. This often happens to someone immersed for long periods of time in the discursive worlds of any particular cultural context; we become numbed to the ways that discursive world constructs our understandings of the world. In essence, we come to believe that we understand the parables told in a given cultural context, and we forget, as suggested in the epigraph to this chapter, that parables can be told in multiple ways with different definitions of "winning or losing."

We naturalize our understandings of environmental "issues" and forget that our understandings are smoothed and sanded by the grit and friction of our cultural ideas. In fact, in our scientifically based society, we tend to think that our understandings of the environment, and the proper ways to manage it, are immune to culture. Undercutting this kind of unexamined assumption is one of the most valuable contributions that an anthropological consciousness can make.

The anthropological record, in fact, suggests a direct critique of contemporary environmental narratives: As work on local people's conceptions of their ecology (ethnoecology) has shown, technical concepts are not merely utilitarian but embedded in broader sets of ideas and beliefs—ways of thinking about and understanding the world. Whether environmental processes and phenomena have a material existence in and of themselves, anthropology stresses that the meanings that people impose on them are always socially and culturally shaped (Leach and Fairhead 2002, 210).

Although Saraguro is remote geographically from the Great Lakes, Benigno's stories grapple with some of the same realities of the contemporary world, and the way stories are told in Saraguro can illuminate different ways of expressing these realities. In a small but significant way I want to use my reading of these Saraguro stories to create havoc with my own and fellow environmentalists' settled ways of thinking and conceptualizing, to challenge the received wisdoms in our own *leyendas* with what I see as a more *matizada* perspective.

A SCIENTIFIC *LEYENDA*: SMOOTHING A PATH FOR TRAVELING, PARASITIC FISH IN THE SWEETWATER SEAS

The fish community in Lake Michigan—and to a lesser extent Lake Superior—has changed dramatically over the last 100 years largely due to the introduction of exotic species.

One of the greatest impacts on the Great Lakes has been the eel-like sea lamprey, which is native to the Atlantic Ocean. It made its way past Niagara Falls via the Welland Canal by the 1920s, and colonized Lake Michigan in the 1930s and Lake Superior in the 1940s.

The effect of the sea lamprey on lake trout, whitefish and other large bodied species was devastating, explains Bill Horns, a DNR [Department of Natural Resources] Great Lakes fisheries biologist.

For example, before the lamprey invasion of Lake Superior, the lake trout harvest averaged about 4.5 million pounds; by 1960, it was less than 500,000 pounds. The lamprey is a parasitic species that feeds on the body fluids of other fish by attaching itself to a fish with its sucker-like mouth and rasping a hole in the body. Fish that survive those attacks often have scars to prove it. But only one in seven fish survives a lamprey attack. Each adult lamprey can consume 40 pounds of fish a year. Along with harvest by commercial fishing and habitat degradation, lamprey contributed to the extermination of lake trout in all the Great Lakes, except Superior.

In response to the lamprey invasion, the Great Lakes Fishery Commission was created in 1954 and given authority to implement a binational sea lamprey control program. The commission developed a program that uses barriers to block the migration of adult sea lamprey upstream to spawn, uses a selective lampricide (known as TFM) to kill larval sea lamprey, sterilizes males, and is studying the use of pheromones to lure adult lamprey into traps.

By the 1960s, the sea lamprey control program had reduced sea lamprey abundance by 90 percent to the point where large fish such as lake trout, salmon, burbot and whitefish once again thrived in the Great Lakes. This opened the door to fish stocking and resurgence of sport and commercial fisheries. Yet, this parasite still takes about half as much of the lean lake trout from Lake Superior as do sport and commercial fishing, emphasizing the need to continue sea lamprey control. Sea lamprey control costs taxpayers $15 million annually.

Like the lamprey, alewives gained access to Lake Michigan through the Welland Canal. The first documented report was in 1949. Because lamprey had collapsed the lake trout populations in Lake Michigan in the 1950s, there were no predators to control alewives. In Lake Michigan, the alewife population became too large to support in the 1960s and 70s, resulting in huge dieoffs. Some will recall beaches littered with piles of silvery dead alewives in places such as Milwaukee. The abundant alewives may have hurt some native species including yellow perch.

In 1966 fish biologists turned to coho salmon and stocked them in Lake Michigan as alewife predators, and followed by stocking chinook salmon, brown trout, and rainbow trout.

"It's an example of controlling an exotic with another exotic," Horns notes.

"Alewives are held in check primarily by the chinook salmon, which is also not native to Lake Michigan." (Kassulke 2001)

On the surface, the story of the invasion of the sea lamprey appears to have the same message as Benigno's parables—messing with the natural order of things leads to dangerous consequences. However, the scientific tale outlines clear cultural parameters that suggest an approach to ecological imagination very different from that in Benigno's stories. Of significant note, the lamprey story revolves around science as a distancing tool through which the citadel of technocratic control claims the ground for understanding and manipulating the natural and social worlds. The story of the sea lamprey focuses on gathering and disseminating scientific data as well as the cost to the economy and taxpayers, reflecting the instrumentality common to modern, technocratic societies rather than the relationality of humans with their environment. This cultural pattern is not isolated in the Great Lakes to the historical case of the lamprey but continues to the present with recurrent waves of scientific management approaches to new invasive species such as the Asian carp, zebra mussel, round goby, and others. As with the trout in Benigno's stories, it is a traveling species of fish, animals "not-of-this-place," that illuminates cultural parameters for human action in relation to the ecology of the place.

Note that the story, as related here, mystifies the human agency that has set the conditions for the invasion of the lamprey. Except for the intervention of scientists in restoration efforts, the invasion, though spurred by the construction of canals, seems to have taken place as if an implacable force of nature has moved along understandable and predictable paths. Perhaps because of the scale and time span of the invasion, the story that gets told of lampreys is detached from specific human actors and institutions such as companies that build canals and the regulatory state and is cast in the accounting language of an instrumental science. No individuals or institutions are named as culpable in the invasion, and despite the assertion that "it [the lamprey] made its way past Niagara Falls via the Welland Canal by the 1920s," no specific moments are really identified as part of the process. The complex social history of corporate and state decision making and social labor to turn the Great Lakes into part of the nation's transportation infrastructure is reduced to a side comment.

In fact, the description of the spread of this exotic species focuses almost exclusively on a scientific description of the animal and its feeding properties ("The lamprey is a parasitic species that feeds on body fluids of other fish by attaching itself to a fish with its sucker-like mouth and rasping a hole in the body. Fish that survive those attacks often have scars to prove it. But only one in seven fish survives a lamprey attack. Each adult lamprey can consume 40 pounds of fish a year"), as well as an analysis of the economic effects of the lamprey's invasion ("For example, before the lamprey invasion of Lake Superior, the lake trout harvest averaged about 4.5 million pounds; by 1960, it was less than 500,000 pounds").

In all of this, the human role in, and therefore accountability for, the spread of the lamprey is basically minimized. The major focus of specific human agency is on the scientists who are working on restoration efforts.

In response, it is worth underscoring that the role of science is not simply a scientific discourse but also a moral one. Robin Grove-White, for example, highlights the role of an "orthodox consensus" version of scientific environmentalism as a moral discourse in contemporary technological society:

> What are the features of this "orthodox" consensus? First, and overwhelmingly, the most pressing problems have been seen as existing objectively in nature, mediated through the natural sciences. Environmental problems worthy of the name are thus regarded as physical problems, arising from specific human interventions in natural systems; their character and boundaries are, so to speak, given to us from nature, their authenticity guaranteed by natural scientific investigation and confirmation (with global population pressures adding a chronic dimension). This being the case, the argument continues, what we need now are "solutions" to mitigate these physically identified "problems"—solutions which may be found in persuasion or regulation, in technological innovation, in international agreements, or in the application of economic instruments. (1993, 19–20)

This consensus, Grove-White argues, has four significant shortcomings: "(1) trivializing the public's role, (2) inflating the role of science, (3) the 'perverse dominance' of a reliance on 'interests' as the central tool for explaining environmental concern or value, and (4) inadequate or superficial treatment of the mysteriousness and open-endedness of existence" (ibid., 20–25). All four of these shortcomings of orthodox technocratic environmentalism as a moral discourse can be clearly seen in the myth of the sea lamprey invasion conveyed above. They also run in direct contrast to the *matizada* ecological imagination embedded in Benigno's leyendas.

The contemporary story of lamprey invasion and control suggests that at least on the imaginative level, the management of natural resources in the United States has not significantly progressed from the basic ecological imagination that helped to construct such wildlife management mistakes as that of the Kaibab deer herd in Arizona. In this early example (beginning in 1905) of applying science to wildlife management, the deer herd in the Kaibab forest of Arizona was cultivated to maximize "productivity." Predators such as wolves and cougars were exterminated from the area. The predictable (in hindsight) result was that the herd increased from an ebb of four thousand to a peak of one hundred thousand in an eighteen-year span, to the celebratory applause of management technocrats. Over the next decade, however, the population plummeted again to ten thousand because of limitations apparently inherent in the grazing capacity of the range.

The "solution," of course, was more management, not less. Rather than allowing populations of predators to rebound naturally, humans took on the role of top predators: "The deer, it was now agreed, had to be kept within the carrying capacity of their range. But this was a job the human hunters could perform as well as the vanquished predator, and they were most eager to undertake it. Thus a new man-made ecological order came to exist on the Kaibab Plateau, as elsewhere in America—an ecological order engineered by wildlife managers and requiring their perpetual supervision" (Worster 1977, 271).

I am not suggesting that wildlife scientists respond to contemporary issues, such as the sea lamprey invasion, the same way the deer managers in the Kaibab did, but I argue that the underlying ecological imagination is not very different. In both cases the approach to dealing with aspects of ecological relationships as resources revolves around a political practice that accepts the ability of scientific humans to understand and intervene in ecological processes. Moreover, this intervention takes place without acknowledging responsibility for the causes of disruption. Instead, the focus is on science as the instrumental tool for redressing the "wrongs" that unnamed past humans have inflicted on the environment ("'It's an example of controlling an exotic with another exotic,' Horns notes. 'Alewives are held in check primarily by the chinook salmon, which is also not native to Lake Michigan'"). The primacy of scientific cosmography justifies the marshaling of social and economic resources to support the institutional practices of scientific management.

In contrast, the parables of human activity in the Ecuadorian mountains offer clearly identified actors who behave in individualized ways that have direct repercussions that are both environmental and social. They also include explicit and frequent references to human labor—both individual and collective. Although these are at one level merely storytelling strategies, they also reveal an imagination that is structured by closer proximity to the realities and accountabilities of ecological processes. Benigno and other Saraguros know that they have taken active roles in reshaping the ecological processes of their place—that knowledge leads them to meditate carefully on the relative threats and benefits of such reshaping. In *la vida matizada*, human beings with the ability to act in the world are always one of the blended players in ecological processes.

The sources for this cultural difference in ecological imagination may at least partially be traceable to the distinction between "ecosystem" people and "biosphere" people first developed by Raymond Dasmann (1976) and discussed subsequently by other anthropologists (e.g., Milton 1996; Nadasdy 2005). Dasmann's basic idea is that "ecosystem" people (primarily small-scale, traditional communities that are less significantly caught up in industrial society) rely on the resources of a single ecosystem, whereas "biosphere" people (large-scale, industrial societies) draw on the resources of the entire biosphere. Milton draws out the logical implications of such a distinction: "Insofar as people view their environment anthropocentrically—in terms of its use and value to them—their assessment of its importance will be affected by the extent to which they see themselves as dependent upon it. If they do not need it for their own survival and comfort, they are less likely to be concerned if it is threatened" (1996, 137). If the health of your livelihood *blends* with the health of the environment in clearly perceivable ways, you are more likely to think about how you interact with the resources you use from that environment.

This distinction, however, only goes part of the way in explaining the different moral centers of these stories. Contemporary Saraguros do not fit neatly into a box that reads "Ecosystem Peoples." As part of a globalized system, contemporary Saraguro subsistence strategies draw locally on more than one ecosystem—many families integrate pastoral activities that depend on resources beyond their immediate environment (the recently colonized rainforest, for example) for economic benefit, as well as draw on fluid economic strategies (such as migration and remittance of income) in the larger global economy.

This being the case, there must be other cultural reasons for the differences in these two kinds of stories. Here, it is worth pointing out that the phenomenon of a "soft," "weak," or "integrated" form of dualism has long been noted for many highland Andean cultures. The apparent ambiguity in Benigno's stories about trout underscores an ethnographically described cosmology that refuses to see most aspects of the world as purely good or bad but, rather, sees change as mixed and contingent in its outcomes for human society.

For example, Carpenter (1992) documents linguistic patterns in Andean

Quechua of conceptions of self as dual but not dichotomized. In Quechua, according to Carpenter, the "self" is composed of an internal component that is private and uncontrollable and an external component that is public and controllable. His research indicates that the two parts coexist and are not separable, much like the model of complementarities suggested by the Taoist "yin–yang" symbol. Carpenter writes: "These components are closely tied to each other and not in opposition, as they are in many European cultures. This allows for freedom of movement between the two and helps to maintain both components in harmony, ensuring the individual's well-being. It is so basic that Quechua speakers assume it is a natural part of everyone's existence" (Carpenter 1992, 130). In the chapter on women's cooperatives, I outlined some of the ways this complementary dualism relates to gender relations in Saraguro. With such a worldview, it seems unlikely that something as complex as the introduction of a useful exotic species (and all the attendant benefits and challenges thereof) would be interpreted as altogether a positive or negative cultural fact. Here, again, a preference for *matizada*, for an understanding of reality as blended, reveals itself.

The differences between the Saraguro and Great Lakes stories are not static distinctions. The stories Benigno told are not "ancient stories of a primitive people"—they are stories created in the last fifty years that draw in fluid ways on multiple aspects of the contemporary situation in Ecuador. As such, they are not classic or nostalgic folktales but nuanced thinking about current issues. In fact, the stories told about the invasion by sea lampreys are actually more static—the basic contours of the ecological imagination that underlies this technocratic story of scientific management of invasive species parallel those of one-hundred-year-old stories such as that of the scientific management of the Kaibab Plateau ecosystem. The purpose of management has shifted in the lamprey case to managing for restoration, but the basic approach—that only scientific knowledge can adequately assess and deal with environmental "problems" and that the public's proper role is to assume the passive role of adequately supporting the efforts of activist scientists—reveals the same underlying imagination at play.

IMPLICATIONS FOR ACTION AND INACTION
ON ENVIRONMENTAL ISSUES

Milton (1996, 136–137) contends that the key to whether individuals or institutions within a culture respond directly and effectively to concern for the environment hinges less on the level of scientific knowledge in the society than it does on cultural issues such as the perceived balance of power in human–environment relations, the perception of whether the environment is fragile or resilient, and the question of whether the environment is seen as something valuable to be protected. It is these key cultural, rather than strictly scientific, questions that this interpretation of ecological imaginations explores. In this interpretive task, the question of where moral authority lies in a particular cultural context is significant:

> We may need to ask other questions to determine the likelihood of their [a specific population] actually adopting environmental principles. For instance, how is moral responsibility allocated within the society? People who acknowledge that they have the power to protect the environment, and that it is important to do so, might still see it as someone else's responsibility. . . . Within a liberal democracy, the public and the government tend to delegate responsibility to each other. The public assumes that they elected the government for that very purpose, while the government tends to treat an apparent lack of public concern as reason not to act; they act only when public protest or voting patterns prompt them to do so. (1996, 137–138)

In the two versions of ecological imaginations outlined above, the centers of responsibility are very different. In the stories of Benigno Cango, the locus of moral responsibility lies with local-level communities — when individuals act in disruptive ways, the entire community is brought to task, directly and powerfully. However, in the scientific myth of the sea lamprey invasion, the diffusion of moral responsibility creates an abstracted tale that holds no direct moral lessons for human behavior other than the implicit idea that science needs our support to solve problems, underscoring the idea of science as citadel.

Saraguros are not intrinsically better or worse thinkers about ecology than the environmental scientists and environmental activists that I have been working with and around for the last fifteen years. However, thinking carefully and comparatively about cultural inflections in the ways that we exercise our ecological imaginations brings significant benefits.

When we tell stories about our society's place within ecological processes that remove the role of specific humans and specific human activities, we step away from *la vida matizada* into a realm of abstractions about scientific processes. Without a sense of the woven togetherness of our actions and the ecological realities we live within, it is difficult to engage with environmental issues in direct ways.

For instance, North American environmental activists often point to the fact that despite polling results indicating high levels of broad environmental concern (at various times, up to three-fourths of U.S. citizens have claimed they are environmentalists; see Kempton, Boster, and Hartley 1995), these sentiments rarely translate to action to deal with environmental dilemmas. One could attribute this to apathy or unwillingness to budge from positions of privilege and comfort. Or one could acknowledge that possibility while also examining the imaginaries available in the stories we offer of environmental science and activism.

Is there enough imaginative body in these stories to reach citizens on a concrete, direct level? If we abstract our ecological imaginations, if we separate the insights of science from blending with the insights we have from daily life, we make room primarily for abstract, perhaps ultimately ineffective, environmental platitudes about the importance of conservation. Without *la vida matizada* approach to the story, without a sense of the blending of our lives with nonhuman others, there are few opportunities for individuals to understand how our culture's actions ramify in ecological systems we depend on.

Meanwhile, we leave distant technocrats and bureaucrats to wrangle about "problems" and "solutions" while fierce storms of other not-of-this-place animals and plants follow the same limited environmental and story paths to the "Sweetwater Seas" of the Great Lakes and elsewhere.

Interlude 4

EMPTY DOORWAYS AND SHADOWY FIGURES: ANTHROPOLOGIST AS ACCIDENTAL BUSINESS CONSULTANT

The economic crises of Ecuador at the turn of the millennium have made life much more difficult for all Saraguros—perhaps most of all for those pursuing new strategies that more immediately depend on national and global conditions than did the traditional Saraguro focus on agropastoralism.

LUIS MACAS, LINDA BELOTE, AND JIM BELOTE, "INDIGENOUS DESTINY IN INDIGENOUS HANDS," IN *MILLENIAL ECUADOR*, EDITED BY NORMAN E. WHITTEN JR. (2003)

Tourism, increasingly common as both practice and development policy, engages culture and nature in myriad ways. Tagged with an "eco" prefix, it accumulates new meanings associated with sustainability and environmental responsibility. But as the "eco" enjoinder presses individuals, institutions and communities to preserve and protect the environment, the actual practice of ecotourism continuously pries open new spaces into which physical bodies and cultural meanings flow. The result is mutability rather than sustainability, where local nature is reordered as global commodity, and local meanings are reinterpreted to better align with consumers' desires.

FRANK HUTCHINS, "FOOTPRINTS IN THE FOREST: ECOTOURISM AND ALTERED MEANINGS IN ECUADOR'S UPPER AMAZON" (2007)

Rosa Medina Sarango in her traditional Saraguro clothing.

"WE LIVE VERY HUMBLY; we don't have much," said Rosa Medina Sarango when I first visited her home. "We cannot even afford enough doors for our house."

Rosa and her husband, José, have three children ranging in ages from four to thirteen. They live in a multifloored, but unfinished, house that they are completing as they secure resources to pay for materials. It is a slow process.

As a member of Las Calcutas women's cooperative, and an accomplished beadworker, Rosa contributes to her family's economic resources through artisanal work, as well as through agricultural labor. When I got to Rosa's for a conversation about her participation in the Calcutas cooperative, they took me upstairs to the topmost room, set at the apex like a guard station on a castle tower. They had set up a small

Rosa's beading table set up near a second-floor window to take advantage of natural light.

Rosa's son Jonathan is intelligent and talented and often helps with his younger sisters. He gave me copies of his recorded songs, and when I returned another day, I gave him copies of my band's music.

recording studio for Jonathan, their oldest son. The room was a ten-foot by ten-foot cubicle with a computer, a small mixing board, a microphone on a stand, and a guitar leaning in the corner. They wanted to show me a video of Jonathan when he sang a ballad at an event held in honor of President Rafael Correa during a visit to Saraguro. A local production company made the video. A Saraguro man in traditional dress introduced and narrated the video. President Correa spoke briefly to the crowd in Quichua and wore a poncho he had been given. Jonathan sang with a live band accompanying. He was impassioned and strong voiced and conscious of the need to "put the song over" to the crowd. After each verse the crowd gave him a round of enthusiastic applause. Jonathan has won a province-wide music contest for his singing.

"Have you seen the Tuncarta community cemetery?" José wanted to know when we talked after we watched the video.

"No, I haven't," I answered.

"Nearby I also have a seed field of *achira*," he said. "I want to grow enough for a seed crop."

In a *matizada* (blending) that combined an entertaining jaunt for the family, and an impromptu business consultation with me, José's query turned into a three-hour walk to the cemetery, the field, and a spot on the river that José and Rosa recently purchased. The family is ambitious and full of creative potential, but economic opportunities are not abundant locally. José has traveled

Rosa and her daughter above the river.

Interlude: Anthropologist as Business Consultant

José Francisco with a field he has planted in achira, *a cash crop. He hopes to raise capital to create an ecotourist lodge.*

outside the community for work, but at the time of my visit in the summer of 2009 he was where he wanted to be—at home with his family. He had used some of the income he had earned outside the community to purchase additional land, including agricultural fields, and some property nearby along the Hierba Buena River. He has planted the field with *achira* (*Canna edulis*), a 1.5-meter tall flowering plant that is used as an ornamental in other regions. The Incas cultivated this plant. The white-rooted variety can be milled into a soft flour (*chuño*) used to make fine pastries. The plant is propagated, like bananas, from cuttings. José wants to grow a commercial crop of *achira* to generate capital to use in developing his land along the river nearby as a spot for tourism.

José wants to build a rustic hostel on the level land he has on the lip of the river canyon and then make a path with handrails down to a spot on the river by a cave. There he would build a

small shelter, perhaps a foot-bridge over the river, and some rope ladders. Tourists

Rosa climbed the hillside in long skirts and carried her beadwork with her. The women of the community almost always have some kind of handwork such as spinning, knitting, or beading with them when they walk.

could fish, swim, and rock climb. In addition, José could guide them on walks to look at wildflowers, trees, and other plants. He would guide folks up to the *páramo* (the high mountain reaches along the route to the Oriente) to show them places such as Condorcillo and Tres Lagunas—highland lakes also stocked with trout.

"Do you think this is a good place for tourism?" José asked when we were by the river.

"Perhaps it would be attractive to tourists," I said, "maybe if you developed a three-to-four-day tourist package that included a day for looking around at this spot by the river, a day hiking into the *páramo* for sightseeing and fishing, and a day for cultural tourism in Tuncarta."

"We could show them a cultural event," he said, "a fiesta with dancing and music and *chicha* [fermented corn beer]. My mother

The kids are independent. Even Rosa's four-year-old daughter rarely needed help getting down the steep slope.

José Francisco took me to visit his mother's house, a nearly hundred-year-old adobe structure located at a lovely spot looking out over the valley.

Misael (Benigno's son) and Jonathan (José Francisco's son) accompanied us on the visit to the river.

José Francisco asked me to photograph him on these stones. He was dressed in slick, black dress shoes and black dress pants, a white dress shirt, and a black jacket, but this did not slow him down. He climbed places I would not try with my stable hiking boots.

lives in a hundred-year-old house that would be a perfect place for this."

"Perhaps the women who make *artesanías* [traditional crafts] could demonstrate and sell their work, too," I suggested. "You'd need to put up a website offering these opportunities, as most United States and European travelers use the Internet to plan trips."

He agreed enthusiastically. I took many photos to give to him to use should he ever get such a project going. The limitation, of course, is that he doesn't have the capital to build the infrastructure he thinks would be needed.

I asked whether he had thought about approaching a local foundation with a proposal, but he said he does not know anybody at a foundation or how to approach lenders. He asked if I could help him.

"My priority needs to be helping the women's cooperative

with their efforts to build a women's house in the community,"
I said. "Perhaps in the future I could help with your plans."

Along the way we passed a planting of *sango* (*Colocasia escu-lenta*)—a large-leafed edible-rooted plant native to Asia but naturalized to Saraguro. The rock formation nearby reminded José Francisco of a face, and he said there are stories about strange figures visiting the area. This reminded him that we should stop at his sister's house. He wanted his sister to tell me about a shadowy figure she had seen inside the cave long ago. A shadowy male figure with two faces rose out of the water up to his chest. He raised his dark arms, as if to embrace her. She ran from the place with her friends, who had not gone into the cave with her. She has never been back down there. She says this *huaca* (malevolent spirit) might take her if she ever returned.

A planting of sango (Colocasia esculenta) *grew on the steep slope where a spring was bubbling through the scree to provide constant water at the roots. José Francisco said there are stories about strange figures visiting the area.*

The opening to the cave where José Francisco's sister saw a two-faced huaca (*malevolent spirit*) *many years ago.*

CHAPTER SIX

On the Development and Value of
an Anthropological Consciousness

*The experience of cross-cultural living reminds us, not in an
intellectual way, but in a firsthand way—full of wincing, shame, hope
and disappointment (and often laughter, both at us and by us)—that
in fact, we know very little about the way things really are.*

SARAH H. DAVIS, "INTRODUCTION: BECOMING HUMAN,"
IN *BEING THERE* (2011)

*Travel changes the way we imagine our home places. We suddenly
see them as fragile, strange, and worth savoring in new ways. . . .
The landscape, re-visioned through travel, is transferred to become a
moving personal commitment of love. Traveling ideas often stimulate
us in just this way. We see the landscapes we know in relation to other
places; we are moved to change how we think at both local and global
scales. Social movements—including movements to preserve rural
landscapes—grow from traveling forms of activism as well as the
transformation of consciousness.*

ANN LOWENHAUPT TSING, *FRICTION* (2005)

THE CLOWN DOCTORS AND THE SICK CHILDREN

Once, a man entering the middle years of his life—meaning
that he began to realize that even if all went well with his health and his
luck, he was closer to the passage we call death than to the passage we
call birth—traveled to a mountainous country far from his home. As he

understood it, he traveled to this country to carry out part of the work he was assigned in life. The actual arrival was accomplished with a not very perilous journey that took him from his frozen home in the far north to the mountains located somewhere near the middle of the world, by some definitions.

The night he arrived he encountered a band of clown doctors, performers seeking different means for healing than knife and pill. As he entered the inn where he would stay for only one night, the would-be clown healers sat in their clown attire listening to the elder of their group tell stories about poor children in hospitals with only enough beds for some of the sick people. Half of the children slept during the day, and half slept during the night. When the sick children were awake, they sat on the floor beside the beds, staring at the walls, trying not to make any noise lest they wake the other children who were sleeping. The elder planned to take the clown healers to visit the children in that hospital in the morning.

MOST ANTHROPOLOGISTS RELISH THE FREE FLOW OF ideas and images possible in telling and writing stories from their field-work. I am also sure that, for me, the urge to story has been kept alive by years of telling bedtime stories to my daughter and son. I started my adult life thinking that first and foremost I wanted to be a writer, a teller of tales. That is still mostly true, but the joy and challenge of learning about real people and real cultures has connected me firmly with the odd realm of nonfiction today called "ethnography."

Sometimes life unfolds in ways that would hardly be believable in a piece of fiction. The brief story above about the clown doctors is an entry from my field notes. When I arrived in Quito late one night in 2009 to begin a summer research trip, the salon in the hostel where I stayed was full of people dressed in clown costumes. They were compassionate clowns-in-training traveling with Patch Adams, the founder of the Gesundheit Institute's clowning health-care movement (http://patchadams.org). The following morning at breakfast I spoke briefly with Mr. Adams and ex-changed ideas for readings about sustainability and culture. That experi-ence reminded me, yet again, that many agendas lead people to travel and seek out cross-cultural experiences to help them define how they think about and live in the world.

As I look back on the words and ideas drawn together into this book, I realize that I have so many intellectual and emotional agendas at play that the whole thing teeters under the load. Unlike so many ethnogra-phies—both those I admire and those I find problematic—I have not ar-rived at a conclusion that can offer a neat final chapter restating and summarizing what I have been doing. When I wrote my first book, which contained everything I then understood well enough to say about my extended family and the place of the Texas Hill Country, I felt a certain sense of entitlement to say what I wanted and conclude where I wanted, even if it was open-ended, because I was writing about my own life and my own history and my own place. I have tried, in this book, to write in a similarly forthright manner, but now that I am here, at the end of what I feel competent to say about Saraguro lives and my own journeys as an anthropologist, I feel like what I have written comes as the throes of a difficult birth. "Throes" feels like the right word here—a condition of agonizing struggle or trouble.

For me, the point of reading a book—any book, whether it be anthropology, fiction, poetry, science, or whatever—is to meet other human beings (and therefore learn a little more about myself as a human being) and to encounter ideas, images, and feelings that resonate sufficiently with my own experiences and understandings to change me in some way. I hope that what I have written, and what you now have read in these pages, delivers enough in the way of stories, ideas, images, and feelings that you have some sense of how some other people live, think, and feel.

Living and thinking is as simple and complex as breathing—we have lots of ideas about how we do these things. Medical science has one set of stories about how we breathe, and meditation traditions have another. They are not necessarily mutually exclusive, though they do place their emphases and attention in different aspects of this relational transaction between the cells in your lungs and every plant and living creature that has lived on this planet. In both cases, the ideas can have as much or as little relevance to your life as you are willing and capable of allowing— and as much relevance as the person describing the insights of either science or meditation is capable of giving you through words and images. In this book, my efforts at representation have been as strong as I can make them, but they are partial and incomplete. To paraphrase a translation of the poet Rumi, what you have been eating is bread made from the flour of your own imagination; I have just tried to add some yeast to the dough.

TO STEP AWAY FROM MIXED METAPHORS OF PLANTS, lungs, flour, and yeast, and to get off a lofty-sounding goal of evoking cross-cultural understanding and compassion, I want to return to the beadwork. Ana Victoria has been doing beadwork and other handwork for twenty-five years or more, and she has been doing it *as if her life depended on it*—because it has. Luis Macas, with Linda and Jim Belote (Macas, Belote, and Belote 2003, 236), relates a saying from Saraguro: "Maquica ruracun, shimaca rimacun" (The hands make and the mouth talks). Macas and the Belotes report that to the Saraguros this saying has a number of meanings, including that one should engage the world with the whole body and being, not just one part of oneself. This spirit of always doing something as if your life were at stake is something I have learned from Ana Victoria and Benigno and the other people I have spent time with in Saraguro. In reflecting on the way that my friends in Saraguro simply *do* the things of their lives with their full effort, I am reminded of a Gary Snyder poem:

WHY LOG TRUCK DRIVERS RISE
EARLIER THAN STUDENTS OF ZEN

In the high seat, before-dawn dark,
Polished hubs gleam
And the shiny diesel stack
Warms and flutters
Up the Tyler Road grade
To the logging on Poorman creek.
Thirty miles of dust.

There is no other life. (Snyder 1992, 244)

It is so easy for people living in rapid-paced, wealthy societies to forget these five words, "There is no other life." In societies with wealth we have so many options for distraction—what we call entertainment—that living each moment as if it matters can easily slip away. My friends in Saraguro approach life with a different emphasis, what I have in this book called *la vida matizada*, which for me has come to mean "the blended life" and also "life paid attention to." Whether it is literally dancing all night to celebrate the graduation of a young man from high school; making pieces of beautiful, wearable art with your hands to earn your economic survival; climbing a coco tree with nothing but a few pieces of rope, some lengths of stick, the strength of your body, and trust in your own knowledge—each of these things should be approached as if your life depends on it—because it does. These moments *are* your life. These are the only moments you will have to live. Living each one fully and with joy, because each one won't be back—this to me is one simple message of *la vida matizada*. For me, it is the constant technopelli work of developing and renewing a full and present consciousness that brings me hope of living in this fully present and open manner.

La vida matizada is a metaphor grounded in webs of practices and meanings I have encountered in my explorations with Saraguro people, but it is, ultimately, an ideal that none of us have fully attained—not Benigno, who tells wonderful and important stories and provides a remarkable stability to a large network of family; not Ana Victoria, whose accomplished craftwork and competent organizing has helped create viable and lasting institutions in her community; not Maximo, who has gained a measure of economic stability and prestige through his hard work in transnational settings; and not myself, whose small talent with words and observation has led me to a career in an academic field I had never heard of until I was nearly an adult. We all aspire to living full, blended, good lives, and we sometimes approach it. But strong forces in our globalizing world revolve around extracting surplus value out of human lives, and the result is that most of us work harder and longer than we want to work, often for less return than our work merits. This is true for Benigno and Ana Victoria, who, despite living in the place and within the social networks they desire to live within, still earn less than $10 a day. And it is true for myself, who sometimes teaches two hundred students in an introductory anthropology class, earning the university where I teach four times my annual salary on that single course, one of five classes I teach every year. Only occasionally do I feel resentful at being exploited in this way by the institution that I serve. Teaching in front of a large audience has become another skill I have learned and developed and now weave into the cloth of my anthropological consciousness. I spend a large portion of my work time designing and delivering lessons to develop an anthropological consciousness in the classroom. Since the fieldwork I do regularly emerges in this context, I want to tell a story that comes from that classroom.

STORIES AS TEACHERS

Michael, my undergraduate teaching assistant, stands in front of the hundred and fifty students who showed up for today's lecture on the anthropology of religion. He works hard to be interesting and serious and informed about some of the basic ways that anthropology approaches the study of religion, and as he talks, he tries to explain a version of what he calls a "phenomenological approach" (taking a cue from the anthropology of religion textbook he used to create his lesson plan for the day). He doesn't seem exactly certain what phenomenology means, but his gloss suggests he thinks of it (following E. E. Evans-Pritchard, whom he quotes liberally in his lesson) as an approach that involves examining the phenomena of a religion with an open mindset that seeks its cultural logic rather than seeking to evaluate the truth or falsity of those religious beliefs. He essentially echoes the description of cultural relativism offered by Miles Richardson in his "Anthropologist — The Myth Teller":

> As a tool for research, cultural relativism was a significant advance in ethnography. And it remains so today. It belongs to that set of ethnographic core values that says to take cultures as they come, don't prejudge them, don't impose your own ethnocentric categories upon them. In order to comprehend any item of a people's culture, you have to view that item in its sociocultural context. Cultural relativism is as much a part of the ethnographer's tool kit as are field notes, tape recorders, and cameras. (1975, 523)

Michael sees this relativistic approach as the essence of anthropology's contribution to understanding religion. And he seeks to encourage his fellow undergraduates to practice open-mindedness about the beliefs of others as we explore arguments about Lakota religious beliefs and the status of Devil's Tower in U.S. society. The students look at him with the gaze typical of large lecture classes — some interested and engaged, others half-bored, wondering how any of this relates to them, and, pointedly, calculating what parts of what Michael is saying might be on the test.

"It's important to suspend judgment about religious beliefs different than your own," Michael says, giving the anti-ethnocentric line he has learned from this and other classes in the state university anthropology program where I teach. "It's the best way to try to understand the way religious beliefs work without letting your own beliefs and bias interfere."

As Michael finishes his lecture, I remember a moment from fieldwork in southern Ecuador, and I ask if I can follow Michael's lesson with a story, one to raise some questions about how easy or difficult it is to suspend judgment influenced by one's own beliefs. Michael nods, and I stand up from the seat among the students that I have taken for this class period and tell the following story, spontaneously — I hadn't thought of telling this, or any story, on this day. For the gloss on church history and the conflict over sacred sites that I describe in the story, I depend on the description provided by Linda and Jim Belote in conversation following the ceremony at the cave described below.

"AND THEN THE SHAMAN SPIT
PERFUME IN MY FACE . . ."

Two years ago I traveled to the southern part of Ecuador with a group of fifteen students. A January-term field school was being conducted by the two anthropologists Linda Belote and Jim Belote, who have been visiting the region of Saraguro, Ecuador, for more than fifty years. Everybody in Saraguro knows the Belotes, and they are considered friends by hundreds, perhaps thousands, of people there. I had been told by several Saraguro friends that the Belotes have "amigos en todos lados" (friends on every side). As part of the field school experience, the Belotes arranged for us to attend a ceremony conducted in a cave high on a cliff-side that is sometimes called the "Cave of the Incas." The cave has been one of the sites of contestation between indigenous religious beliefs and the Catholic Church. When Catholicism colonized the area, the cave was identified as a place that needed purification from old religions, and beginning a few hundred years ago, priests from town held an annual mass in the cave. A Christian cross (first wood, more recently reinforced concrete) has occupied a prominent spot in the cave for a long time. The cave was identified as a place over which the Church held power.

Over the centuries, the cave declined in significance to the Church, since the battle against indigenous religions seemed to have been finished long ago. However, in the last decade or so, things have begun to shift. A local revitalization effort has renewed interest in pre-colonial cultural forms among some Saraguros. One man, Carlos, has studied with shamans in the Oriente, the Amazonian lowlands to the east of Saraguro, and has begun practicing in Saraguro as a healer and ritual leader. Other people have begun to follow some of the practices he outlines—practices that are likely a mixture of several cultural traditions of shamanic healing combined with ideas about local history and places of significant power. Carlos and others have reclaimed the cave as a site for religious and medicinal practice. At some point, the metal and concrete cross was destroyed—its only remnant in the cave a tangled mess of rebar sunk into the concrete that was the base.

The priest in the local church, perhaps deferring to on-the-ground realities significantly different from those of past times, did not really try to fight the reclaiming of the cave for other religious practices. He did comment in sermons that the Devil had returned to the cave (which in some stories is the local Mouth of Hell), as could be seen by the lights that sometimes danced on the trail up to and inside the cave at night. One story told by Petrona, Benigno's mother, tells of a wandering man encoun-

141) *Development of an Anthropological Consciousness*

tering three strangers, one of whom turns out to be the Devil. The man goes through various adventures that lead him to the cave, where he gets a glimpse of Hell before being saved by advice from the other two men. Some ceremonies are now being held by candlelight in the cave. But aside from a passing comment in a sermon, the local representatives of the modern Church do not seem overly threatened by the ceremonies of Carlos and others.

This is all the background you need to understand the story I want to tell.

We—the students, the Belotes, and I—climbed up to the cave on a Sunday afternoon. A fairly ambitious walk up a steep path got us to the cave in about thirty minutes. Carlos led us into the cave, which is perhaps twenty to thirty yards deep, three times as long, and broadly open at its mouth, giving the effect more of a cliff shelter like those in the U.S. Southwest than a darkened cave.

Carlos had prepared his ritual objects prior to our arrival. He had arranged a collection of bottles, flowers, and stones in front of a large, square boulder that he would use as a seat. The boulder, tucked back close to where the ceiling of the cave curves round to become one of its walls, serves Carlos as a place of strength. He identifies this stone and cave as one of his teachers. When he first visited the cave, he found that the stone was just his size; that is, it was the exact distance from the cave ceiling to the stone so that his head made light contact with the ceiling when he sat on the boulder, completing an energetic connection between the above and below.

Carlos told us how he came to have his shamanic powers, learning from the stones and from the earth, and from very powerful healers from the Oriente. His wife, who assists him, hovered nearby and handed him bottles and flowers as he asked for them, while also helping to explain the process to the students. Carlos prayed, sang, and played a traditional Andean end-blown flute called a *quena*. His wife prepared a shell with perfumed smudge materials to be passed around by the group.

Carlos asked whether anyone wanted to receive a private blessing/ prayer. One of the students raised his hand, and Carlos brought him to sit on the ground in front of his seat on the stone. The shaman prayed over the student, sang another song, and smudged him from the material burning in the shell. Then the shaman took a swig from one of the bottles filled with perfumed water and spit it into the student's face as a fine spray. The student winced a bit and closed his eyes. The sweet, floral smell filled the area of the cave where we were clustered.

After a few moments of prayer and singing, Carlos gestured and his wife helped the student to his feet while the shaman asked if there were any others who wanted personal prayers. A few more students braved the process. I also sat down to receive the ceremony, which proceeded along the same lines for each of us—ending with a fine spray of perfume, each receiving a different type, as determined by Carlos's assessment of our needs.

We finished the ceremony, breaking up to look around the cave a bit, and each of us took our thoughts with us as we headed down the steep path. The ceremony had taken about an hour.

Later that night, I was back in the village where I stay with Benigno and Ana Victoria, who knew of Carlos and his shaman's identity. Feeling tired, I went to bed a bit early and woke up in the middle of the night, long after the village sounds suggested most people were asleep. I woke feeling uneasy, feeling a sense of indefinite dread, as if something unknown and ominous were approaching. Down the valley I heard dogs begin to bark, and the sound slowly rolled upward toward the house where I stay. The feeling of dread grew as the sound of the dogs came toward the house where I lay in the dark. It felt as if some cloud of malice were advancing up the road, perhaps intent on reaching where I was or perhaps simply moving through the village to pass on to the next.

At any rate, I felt spooked. Without thinking about it, I pulled a bamboo flute—a Japanese *shakuhachi* I had brought with me to Ecuador—off the bedpost where it was slung, and in the dark played a few notes. I found myself playing a simple melody I had never played before but that sounded like one of the songs Carlos had played earlier in the day. I played softly for a few minutes, the fear and dread eased, the dogs in the valley fell quiet, and I had the sense that the malicious cloud had either dissipated or slid back down the hill to the distant river. I fell asleep.

In the morning, I woke with a raging head cold, which incapacitated me for several days. I was still unused to the altitude, and having a sinus cold significantly reduced my breathing. I stayed close to my "home" and didn't get into the town center or elsewhere for several days. About a week later I ran into Carlos on one of the town's two main squares. He asked after my health, and I told him about the cold I was just finishing suffering through. He asked whether anything had happened after the ceremony a week earlier, and when I explained the events of that night as best as I could, he nodded.

"I thought something like that had happened," he said, not offering any further explanation. After another minute of small talk we went our separate ways.

A few months after those events, when I returned for summer research in Saraguro, I met with Carlos to give him a letter from a former student who had stayed with him during the Belotes' field school a few years earlier. We chatted briefly after I gave him the letter, and I told him I would carry a return letter for him if he wanted. He thanked me and said he would write one. Carlos asked what I was studying while in Saraguro, and I told him I was learning beadwork from Ana Victoria but that I also hoped to write a more general book about the time I spend with the Saraguros. He wanted to know what I planned to write about, and seemed suspicious of me. I understood his suspicion — he seems critical of the fact that anthropologists have the power to shape perceptions of the Saraguros in the larger world. His wariness shapes the anthropological consciousness I bring to my stories and writing.

STORYTELLING AND IMPROVISATION IN CREATING AN ANTHROPOLOGICAL CONSCIOUSNESS

So that was the story, more or less, as I told it to a lecture hall of undergraduates, and where a few minutes before they had been rather passively absorbing what their teaching assistant was telling them about the need for suspending judgment to understand other cultures, now they were waiting for me to step out of the storyteller's role and explain the story to them. What was in that perfume? Did I think the ceremony really stirred up some malevolent energy? Did I believe the shaman had power? What did it all mean?

"I know that I perceived what I am describing in the manner I am describing it," I said. "I know what I experienced that night, at least in the subjective sense of really feeling fear and having it go away when I played that song on my flute."

"Other than that, I know that it is not so easy to set aside your own belief systems and cultural training. It's a process that you either do or don't do, at the moment that something happens to you that doesn't seem comprehensible using your usual set of explanations. I'm not a believer in shamanism, per se, but I also know I can't just chalk that experience up to my imagination. It is what it is, an experience of something outside my usual worldview. Something that challenges me to open my consciousness to a different mode of perceiving the world."

The students came away with a small piece of experience about the complex ways that one's own cultural context shapes any attempt to consider the cultural context of another human being. When I finished my story, the large lecture hall, home to so many shufflings, text messagings, whispers, yawns, and boredoms, was silent as an untapped drum, waiting for a stick or hand to strike the next beat. That attunement of receptive experience, ready for what comes next in the education of the social self, represents the kernel of an anthropological consciousness. It is something that I, as a regular teacher of large undergraduate classes, relish in its infrequent, mostly unpredictable manifestations.

The story I told in that course *worked*, in at least two senses of the word. It worked as a means of accomplishing a goal—shaking these students momentarily out of passive intellectual torpor—*and* it made an impact on the conception that the people in the room, including myself, have of what an anthropological consciousness is. The students got a small glimmer of the challenges to thought and feeling that one often encounters in carrying out fieldwork, and the telling of that story helped me to find another focal point for understanding how fieldwork continuously shapes and reshapes my own anthropological consciousness.

TWO OR THREE THINGS I KNOW FOR SURE ABOUT *LA VIDA MATIZADA* AND THE TECHNOPELLI

After the stories are told, my students look to me to draw forth meaning from what has been told. This, finally, is the responsibility of the technopelli: to exchange stories with people and to carry, tell, and interpret them in multiple contexts. The title of this final section echoes an essay by Dorothy Allison (1995), a storyteller who has been a continuous inspiration for me as I have made my way from the insecurity of an abusive, working-class childhood into my current academic life as an anthropology professor. Her lessons to me as a writer have been many, but one of them is that finally, the storyteller must come clean about what she or he understands in the stories.

So, two or three things I know for sure about *la vida matizada*:

La vida matizada is the blended life. It is also the blended necklace where only certain colors constitute "blending." Other colors may look good together to an outsider or may have a "rainbow" effect in the pattern, but they are still not *matizada*. The relations of *matizada* become most clear when I am in the flow of the *matizada* life that I and Benigno and Ana Victoria and others express a desire for. I see it most clearly when I am reflecting on the metaphor and its practice in beadwork, the specific colors that create *matizada* appearing to be those colors assigned to the concept of tradition—which is really a historically *new* lifeway that emerges at the intersections of transnationalism and notions of indigenous identity and the good life. What counts as *matizada* for Saraguro people has changed and will change over time, but the idea remains continuously cogent — what counts as *matizada* shifts and is rewoven as people reflect on their present lives and their relationships to inherited ideas. What counts as tradition has no real, objective past and no real future — it primarily has an ongoing, negotiated presence in the now.

When I ask the women to explain to me why a color combination is or is not *matizada*, they don't really want to explain it — most often they turn it into a joke ("We don't use white, because we are black.") But they know what *matizada* is and that it is good because it is *matizada* — a tautology that the good life is good because it is the life that is good for them in this time and in this place.

And finally, two or three things I know for sure about the technopelli: the technopelli is a person who notices these things. Unlike the cyborg, the technopelli is not *reliant* on technologies to do his or her work; rather, the technopelli engages with the etymological undertones of *technology* present in the Greek notion of *technē*, often rendered as "craftsmanship" or, more vaguely, as "art." Inherent in *technē* is making and doing. The technopelli is the anthropologist who spends hours of an afternoon beading and learning from someone willing to teach him or her *matizada* as it manifests in the beadwork. In the making and doing (not only of beadwork, but digging, fishing, planting, talking with families trying to make better lives for themselves, and walking, walking, and more walking), the technopelli notices *matizada* in many arenas: the ways that certain ideas and actions allow a good life to be fostered by the people when they can avoid transnational expeditions to gain livelihood by labor in other lands, the ways that children are deeply cared for and allowed tremendous independence, the ways that stories blend animals and people as they move toward truth, the ways that asking questions and taking notes does not remain the singular terrain of the ethnographer. Anthropological consciousness moves and flows with *matizada*, and the technopelli becomes acutely aware of this in the making and doing of anthropological work.

And the technopelli is asked to do things: eat this, drink that, write this, fix that problem with transnationalism, create opportunities for the exchange of goods. The technopelli can't resolve these frictions, but he or she can render them visible. The global connections Tsing writes about that make capitalism, science, and politics possible also rely heavily on high levels of invisibility for indigenous people and for the joys, struggles, and sufferings of everyday life. Global capitalism does not attend to suffering; we know this. It encourages us, its denizens, to think that domestic work, growing food, making craft, raising children, and the myriad other tasks and joys of creating a good life are insignificant in the dizzying daily flows of money.

With notepad, beading needle, and voice recorder, the technopelli notices the frictions, tells the stories of *matizada*, of humans with an anthropological consciousness negotiating the topographies, beauties, challenges, and weathers of their lives in the contemporary world.

Epilogue

A STORY FOR A TECHNOPELLI'S
LAST HOUR IN TOWN

"*L*ET'S GO SEE ONE MORE PLACE," BENIGNO SAYS.
"I have one more story for David's last hour in Tuncarta
for now."

I thought the walk with Benigno, which I describe in the prologue of this book, was the end of my research trip in the summer of 2009, but, as suggested in the thoughts at the end of our conversation during that walk, the learning never seems to end. On my final morning, after we ate breakfast we had about an hour left before it was time to catch the bus in Saraguro.

We walk up the road, passing his neighbor Angel, who stretches a hose to begin flooding a pile of dirt he is going to make into adobe blocks. We shake hands and I say goodbye to Angel, whom I have met but never really talked with.

Behind the hill, Benigno points out a marshy spot where a small pond seethes with large tadpoles and near-frogs.

"This whole area used to be a lake," he says. "The grandfather of my grandmother knew the story of what happened here. It's not a tale, but a real story of something that happened."

"One night, late, a young boy, about ten years old, was walking his family's sheep home on that path right there." He points to the stone-lined path that is still in place, though the newer road is only about twenty yards beyond it. "He was walking just at this place, when the sheep started bleating, and they startled, and ran as fast as they could to get away from the lake. The lake was full of waves, like on the ocean, and the waves came out of the lakebed and tried to grab the boy and pull him in. He ran, really scared, to his house. 'Papi! The lake tried to grab me,' he said. His father knew then that there was a *huaca* [animating spirit or force, often malevolent] in that lake. The next day he brought an offering of *cuye asado* [grilled guinea pig] with salt and put it right there, over there on the hill for the *huaca*. But the *huaca* didn't like the offering, and the waves kept splashing and crashing on the hillside. The father went back to the house and got a whip. He came back and he lashed the waves with the whip, telling the *huaca* to leave. A great cloud lifted up out of the water and floated off down the hill, carrying most of the water and the *huaca* with it. Ever since, this hasn't really been a lake—just that small pond there, and a marsh filled with these reeds."

Here Benigno grabs a handful of the four-foot spikes of the water plants at the edge of the marsh.

"They're called *lluzhinplan*—that's what the lake was called, and now this place is still called *lluzhinplan.*"

We look around, and I feel the way that this community swells with powers embedded in places. Benigno is a pragmatic, realistic man, with eyes and ears that hear and see multiple dimensions in the inhabited landscape around him—the stories tie him to the flow of times and places that are not only what lies in front of our eyes, but also extends into the past and future.

"This isn't something made up—a *cuento*," Benigno adds. "This is something that really happened."

"How long ago would this have been?" I ask.

He thinks for a moment, calculating the years of his grandmother's grandfather's life. "About two hundred years," he says.

We start back down the road. It is time to drive to town for the bus. While we walk, we talk about the next time I come to visit. Benigno has been collecting stories like this for years—says he has enough of them to fill a fat book.

"We'll work on that book next time," I say. "I have a program on my computer we can use to lay it out and prepare it for printing. Maybe we can publish it in a bilingual edition, like the Neruda book we were reading the other night."

Benigno thinks this is a fine idea and, like me, seems to look forward to the opportunity to work together the next time I put on my pack and we slip together into the roles of the technopelli.

References

Abu-Lughod, Lila. 1993. *Writing Women's Worlds: Bedouin Stories*. Berkeley: University of California Press.

Allen, Catherine. 2002. *The Hold Life Has: Coca and Cultural Identity in an Andean Community*. 2nd ed. Washington, DC: Smithsonian Books.

Allison, Dorothy. 1995. *Two or Three Things I Know for Sure*. New York: Penguin Books.

Applebaum, Herbert. 1992. *The Concept of Work: Ancient, Medieval and Modern*. Albany: State University of New York Press.

Apt Russel, Sharman. 1991. *Songs of the Flute Player: Seasons of Life in the Southwest*. Reading, MA: Addison-Wesley.

Bacacela, Sisapacari. 2003. "La migracíon en los Saraguros: Aspectos positivos y negativos." *Boletín ICCI-ARY Rimay* 5, no. 48 (March).

Bastien, Joseph. 1978. *Mountain of the Condor: Metaphor and Ritual in an Andean Ayllu*. St. Paul: West Publishing.

Behar, Ruth. 1993. *Translated Woman: Crossing the Border with Esperanza's Story*. Boston: Beacon.

————. 1997. *The Vulnerable Observer: Anthropology That Breaks Your Heart*. Boston: Beacon.

Behar, Ruth, and Deborah A. Gordon, eds. 1996. *Women Writing Culture*. Berkeley: University of California Press.

Belote, James. 1984. "Changing Adaptive Strategies among the Saraguros of Southern Ecuador." Ph.D. diss., Department of Anthropology, University of Illinois at Urbana–Champaign.

Belote, Linda. 1978. "Prejudice and Pride: Indian-White Relations in Saraguro, Ecuador." Ph.D. diss., Department of Anthropology, University of Illinois at Urbana–Champaign.

————. 2003. "Ecuadorian Bead Weaving." *Bead and Button* 49:88–89.

Belote, Linda, and Jim Belote. 1981. "Development in Spite of Itself: The Saraguro

Case." In *Cultural Transformations and Modern Ecuador*, edited by Norman E. Whitten Jr., 450–476. Urbana: University of Illinois Press.

————. 1984a. "Drain from the Bottom: Individual Ethnic Identity Change in Southern Ecuador." *Social Forces* 63, no. 1: 24–50.

————. 1984b. "Suffer the Little Children: Death, Autonomy, and Responsibility in a Changing 'Low Technology' Environment." *Science, Technology and Human Values* 9, no. 4: 35–48.

————. 1999. "The Saraguros, 1962–1997: A Very Brief Overview." www.saraguro .org/overview.htm, accessed January 27, 2006.

————. 2005. "Qué hacen dos mil Saraguros en EE.UU. y España?" Paper presented at the FLACSO Conferencia Internacional, "Migración, Transnacionalismo e Identidades: La experiencia ecuatoriana." Quito, Ecuador, January 19.

Berlinger, Joe, dir. 2009. *Crude: The Real Price of Oil*. Entendre Films.

Brown, Karen. 1991. *Mama Lola: A Voudou Priestess in Brooklyn*. Berkeley: University of California Press.

Carpenter, Lawrence K. 1992. "Inside/Outside, Which Side Counts? Duality-of-Self and Bipartization in Quechua." In *Andean Cosmologies through Time*, edited by Robert Dover, Katharine Seibold, and John McDowell, 115–136. Bloomington: Indiana University Press.

Causey, Andrew. 2000. "The Hard Sell: Anthropologists as Brokers in the Global Marketplace." In *Artisans and Cooperatives: Developing Alternative Trade for the Global Economy*, edited by Kimberly L. Grimes and B. Lynne Milgram, 159–174. Tucson: University of Arizona Press.

Center for Latin American Monetary Studies. 2010. "Program for Improving Central Bank Reporting and Procedures on Remittances: Ecuador." Multilateral Investment Fund of the Inter-American Development Bank. http:// idbdocs.iadb.org/wsdocs/getDocument.aspx?DOCNUM=35558629, accessed June 20, 2011.

Cerny, Charlene. 2011. "Market 2011 Wrap Up." www.folkartmarket.org/index.php /blog/entry/market_2011_wrap_up/, accessed August 2, 2011.

Clark, A. Kim, and Marc Becker, eds. 2007. *Highland Indians and the State in Modern Ecuador*. Pittsburgh: University of Pittsburgh Press.

Clifford, James. 1986. "Introduction: Partial Truths." In *Writing Culture: The Poetics and Politics of Ethnography*, edited by James Clifford and George E. Marcus, 1–26. Berkeley: University of California Press.

Clifford, James, and George E. Marcus, eds. 1986. *Writing Culture: The Poetics and Politics of Ethnography*. Berkeley: University of California Press.

Crapanzano, Vincent. 1980. *Tuhami: Portrait of a Moroccan*. Chicago: University of Chicago Press.

Cueva, Edwin. 2005. "Saraguro pierde su identidad." *El Universo*, August 13, 2005.

Dasmann, Raymond. 1976. "Future Primitive: Ecosystem People versus Biosphere People." *CoEvolution Quarterly* 11:26–31.

Davis, Sarah H., and Levin Konner, eds. 2011. *Being There: Learning to Live Cross-Culturally*. Cambridge, MA: Harvard University Press.

Fabian, Johannes. 1983. *Time and the Other: How Anthropology Makes Its Object.* New York: Columbia University Press.

Fox, Richard G., ed. 1991. *Recapturing Anthropology: Writing in the Present.* School of American Research Advanced Seminar Series. Santa Fe, NM: School of American Research Press.

Gardet, L., A. J. Gurevich, A. Kagame, C. Larre, G. E. R. Lloyd, A. Neher, R. Panikkar, G. Pattaro, and P. Ricoeur. 1976. *Cultures and Time.* Paris: UNESCO.

Geertz, Clifford. 1973. "Person, Time, and Conduct in Bali: An Essay in Cultural Analysis." In *The Interpretation of Cultures,* 360–411. New York: Basic Books.

———. 1983. "'From the Native's Point of View': On the Nature of Anthropological Understanding." In *Local Knowledge,* 55–70. New York: Basic Books.

Gordillo, Gaston, and Silvia Hirsch, eds. 2003. "Indigenous Struggles and Contested Identities in Argentina." Special issue, *Journal of Latin American and Caribbean Anthropology* 8, no. 3.

Grimes, Kimberly M., and Lynne Milgram, eds. 2000. *Artisans and Cooperatives: Developing Alternative Trade for the Global Economy.* Tucson: University of Arizona Press.

Grosholz, Emily R. 2007. "On Necklaces." *Prairie Schooner* 81, no. 2 (Summer): 182–195.

Grove-White, Robin. 1993. "Environmentalism: A New Moral Discourse for Technological Society." In *Environmentalism: The View from Anthropology,* edited by Kay Milton, 18–30. ASA [Association of Social Anthropologists] Monographs 32. London: Routledge.

Gualán, Angel Polivio Guamán, and Pedro Manuel Condolo Poma. 2006. *Mitos, cuentos y leyendas del Pueblo Saraguro.* Saraguro: Federacíon Interprovincial de Indígenas Saraguros (FIIS).

Hamre, Keith. 2008. "City of Duluth HUD Income Guidelines." www. duluthmn .gov/planning/cd/cdbg/2008%20HUD%20Income%20Guidelines.pdf, accessed May 5, 2009.

Harris, Olivia. 1978. "Complementarity and Conflict: An Andean View of Women and Men." In *Sex and Age as Principles of Differentiation,* edited by Jean Sybil La Fontaine, 21–40. London: Academic.

Harrison, Jill, Sarah Lloyd, and Trish O'Kane. 2009. "Changing Hands: Hired Labor on Wisconsin Dairy Farms." Briefing no. 1, "Overview of Immigrant Workers on Wisconsin Dairy Farms." www.pats.wisc.edu/final%20dairy%20labor%20briefings.htm, accessed May 9, 2009.

Heckman, Andrea M. 2003. *Woven Stories: Andean Textiles and Rituals.* Albuquerque: University of New Mexico Press.

Herrera, Giocanda, María Cristina Carrillo, and Alicia Torres, eds. 2005. *La migración ecuatoriana: Transnacionalismo, redes e identidades.* Quito: FLACSO.

Hutchins, Frank. 2007. "Footprints in the Forest: Ecotourism and Altered Meanings in Ecuador's Upper Amazon." *Journal of Latin American and Caribbean Anthropology* 12, no. 1: 75–103.

Ingold, Tim. 2011. "On Weaving a Basket." In *The Perception of the Environment: Essays on Livelihood, Dwelling and Skill*, 339–348. London: Routledge.

Isbell, Billie Jean. 1978. *To Defend Ourselves: Ecology and Ritual in an Andean Village*. Austin: University of Texas Press.

Kafka, Franz. 1971. "On Parables." In *The Complete Stories*, edited by N. Glatzer. New York: Schocken Books.

Kassulke, Natasha. 2001. "Tales from the Exotics." *Wisconsin Natural Resources Magazine*. http://dnr.wi.gov/wnrmag/html/supps/2001/jun01/tales.htm, accessed February 18, 2014.

Kempton, Willett, James Boster, and Jennifer Hartley. 1995. *Environmental Values in American Culture*. Cambridge, MA: MIT Press.

Korovkin, Tanya. 1997a. "Indigenous Peasant Struggles and the Capitalist Modernization of Agriculture: Chimborazo, 1964–1991." *Latin American Perspectives* 24, no. 3: 25–49.

———. 1997b. "Taming Capitalism: The Evolution of the Indigenous Peasant Economy in Northern Ecuador." *Latin American Research Review* 32, no. 3: 89–110.

———. 2001. "Reinventing the Communal Tradition: Indigenous Peoples, Civil Society, and Democratization in Andean Ecuador." *Latin American Research Review* 36, no. 3: 37–67.

Kurin, Richard. 1997. *Reflections of a Culture Broker: A View from the Smithsonian*. Washington, DC: Smithsonian Institution Press.

Kyle, David. 2000. *Transnational Peasants: Migrations, Networks, and Ethnicity in Andean Ecuador*. Baltimore, MD: Johns Hopkins University Press.

Lavie, Smadar, Kirin Narayan, and Renato Rosaldo, eds. 1993. *Creativity/Anthropology*. Ithaca, NY: Cornell University Press.

Leach, Melissa, and James Fairhead. 2002. *Exotic No More: Anthropology on the Front Lines*. Chicago: University of Chicago Press.

Lefebvre, Henri. 1987. "The Everyday and Everydayness." *Yale French Studies* 73:7–11.

———. 1991. *The Production of Space*. Translated by Donald Nicholson-Smith. Oxford: Blackwell.

———. 2004. *Rhythmanalysis: Space, Time and Everyday Life*. Translated by Stuart Elden and Gerald Moore. London: Continuum.

Lewellen, Ted. C. 2002. *The Anthropology of Globalization: Anthropology Enters the 21st Century*. Westport, CT: Bergin and Garvey.

Macas, Luis. 1991. *El levantamiento indígina visto por sus protagonistas*. Quito: ICCI.

———. 2000. "The Ecuadorian Indigenous Movement: A Necessary Evaluation." In English: http://icci.nativeweb.org/boletin/21/english.html#macas. In Spanish: http://icci.nativeweb.org/boletin/21/macas.html, accessed June 21, 2011.

Macas, Luis, Linda Belote, and Jim Belote. 2003. "Indigenous Destiny in Indigenous Hands." In *Millennial Ecuador: Critical Essays on Cultural Transformations and Social Dynamics*, edited by Norman E. Whitten Jr., 216–241. Iowa City: University of Iowa Press.

Marcus, George E., and Michael M. J. Fischer. 1986. *Anthropology as Cultural Critique: An Experimental Moment in the Human Sciences*. Chicago: University of Chicago Press.

McKee, Lauris. 1997. "Women's Work in Rural Ecuador: Multiple Resource Strategies and the Gendered Division of Labor." In *Women and Economic Change: Andean Perspectives*, edited by Ann Miles and Hans Buechler, 13–30. Society for Latin American Anthropology Publication Series, vol. 14. Arlington, VA: American Anthropological Association.

McLean, Athena, and Annette Leibing, eds. 2007. *The Shadow Side of Fieldwork: Exploring the Blurred Borders between Ethnography and Life*. Malden, MA: Blackwell.

Meisch, Lynn. 1998a. "Loja Province." In *Costume and Identity in Highland Ecuador*, edited by Ann P. Rowe, 263–271. Seattle: University of Washington Press.

———. 1998b. "Why Do They Like Red? Beads, Ethnicity and Gender in Ecuador." In *Beads and Bead Makers: Gender, Material Culture and Meaning*, edited by Lidia D. Sciama and Joanne B. Eicher, 147–175. Oxford: Berg.

———. 2002. *Andean Entrepreneurs: Otavalo Merchants and Musicians in the Global Arena*. Austin: University of Texas Press.

Miles, Ann. 2004. *From Cuenca to Queens: An Anthropological Story of Transnational Migration*. Austin: University of Texas Press.

Miles, Ann, and Hans Buechler, eds. 1997. *Women and Economic Change: Andean Perspectives*. Society for Latin American Anthropology Publication Series, vol. 14. Arlington, VA: American Anthropological Association.

Milton, Kay. 1996. *Environmentalism and Cultural Theory: Exploring the Role of Anthropology in Environmental Discourse*. London: Routledge.

Munn, Nancy D. 1992. "The Cultural Anthropology of Time." *Annual Review of Anthropology* 21:93–123.

Nadasdy, Paul. 2005. "Transcending the Debate over the Ecologically Noble Indian: Indigenous Peoples and Environmentalism." *Ethnohistory* 52, no. 2: 291–331.

Ogburn, Dennis E. 2008. "Becoming Saraguro: Ethnogenesis in the Context of Inca and Spanish Colonialism." *Ethnohistory* 55, no. 2: 287–319.

Olson, Gary A. 2010. "Why Universities Reorganize." *Chronicle of Higher Education*. August 15. http://chronicle.com/article/Why-Universities-Reorganize/123903, accessed February 10, 2014.

Pelias, Ronald J. 2004. *A Methodology of the Heart: Evoking Academic and Daily Life*. Walnut Creek, CA: AltaMira.

Richardson, Miles. 1975. "Anthropologist — The Myth Teller." *American Ethnologist* 2, no. 3: 517–533.

Rosaldo, Renato, Smadar Lavie, and Kirin Narayan. 1993. Introduction to *Creativity/Anthropology*, edited by Smadar Lavie, Kirin Narayan, and Renato Rosaldo, 1–8. Ithaca, NY: Cornell University Press.

Sawyer, Suzana. 2004. *Crude Chronicles: Indigenous Politics, Multinational Oil, and Neoliberalism in Ecuador*. Durham, NC: Duke University Press.

Shepard, Paul. 1996. *The Others: How Animals Made Us Human*. Washington, DC: Island Press.

Shostak, Marjorie. 1981. *Nisa: The Life and Words of !Kung Woman*. Cambridge, MA: Harvard University Press.

Silverblatt, Irene. 1987 *Moon, Sun, and Witches: Gender Ideologies and Class in Inca and Colonial Peru*. Princeton, NJ: Princeton University Press.

Snyder, Gary. 1992. *No Nature: New and Selected Poems*. New York: Pantheon Books.

Solimano, Andrés. 2003. "Remittances by Emigrants: Issues and Evidence." Report to UN Commission for Latin America and the Caribbean, August 21. http://62.237.131.18/conference/conference-2003-3/conference-2003-3-papers/Solimano-2208.pdf, accessed January 15, 2007.

Stoller, Paul. 2005. *A Stranger in the Village of the Sick: A Memoir of Cancer, Sorcery, and Healing*. Boston: Beacon Press.

———. 2007. "Ethnography/Memoir/Imagination/Story." *Anthropology and Humanism* 32, no. 2: 178–191.

Stoller, Paul, and Cheryl Olkes. 1989. *In Sorcery's Shadow: A Memoir of Apprenticeship among the Songhay of Niger*. Chicago: University of Chicago Press.

Striffler, Steven. 2002. *In the Shadows of State and Capital: The United Fruit Company, Popular Struggle, and Agrarian Restructuring in Ecuador, 1900–1995*. Durham, NC: Duke University Press.

Syring, David. 2000. *Places in the World a Person Could Walk: Family, Stories, Home, and Place in the Texas Hill Country*. Austin: University of Texas Press.

Thompson, E. P. 1967. "Time, Work-Discipline and Industrial Capitalism." *Past and Present* 38 (December 1967): 56–97.

Tilly, Chris, and Charles Tilly. 1998. *Work under Capitalism*. New Perspectives in Sociology. Boulder, CO: Westview.

Toral, Hernan Crespo. 1990. *Saraguro Huasi: La Casa en la Tierra del Maiz*. Quito: Museo del Banco Central Ecuador.

Tsing, Anna. 1993. *In the Realm of the Diamond Queen: Marginality in an Out-of-the-Way Place*. Princeton, NJ: Princeton University Press.

———. 2005. *Friction: An Ethnography of Global Connection*. Princeton, NJ: Princeton University Press.

U.S. Central Intelligence Agency. 2010. "The World Fact Book: Ecuador." www.cia.gov/library/publications/the-world-factbook/geos/ec.html, accessed June 20, 2011.

U.S. Congressional Budget Office. 2005. "Remittances: International Payments by Migrants." www.cbo.gov/ftpdocs/63xx/doc6366/05-19-Remittances.pdf, accessed January 15, 2007.

Vacacela, Alicia. 2002. "La migración indígena." *Boletín ICCI-ARY Rimay* 4, no. 41. http://icci.nativeweb.org/boletin/41/vacacela.html, accessed March 1, 2014.

Vargas-Cetina, Gabriela. 2005. "Anthropology and Cooperatives: From Community Paradigm to the Ephemeral Association in Chiapas, Mexico." *Critique of Anthropology* 25, no. 3: 229–251.

Viatori, Maximilian. 2007. "Zápara Leaders and Identity Construction in Ecuador: The Complexities of Indigenous Self-Representation." *Journal of Latin American and Caribbean Anthropology* 12, no. 1: 104–133.

Walker, Christopher, dir. 1996. *Trinkets and Beads*. Icarus Films.

Waterston, Allise, and Maria D. Vesperi. 2011. *Anthropology off the Shelf: Anthropologists on Writing*. Malden, MA: Wiley-Blackwell.

Weismantel, Mary J. 1988. *Food, Gender, and Poverty in the Ecuadorian Andes*. Philadelphia: University of Pennsylvania Press.

———. 1996. "Time, Work-Discipline, and Beans: Indigenous Self-Determination in the Northern Andes." In *Women and Economic Change: Andean Perspectives*, edited by Ann Miles and Hans Buechler, 31–54. Society for Latin American Anthropology Publication Series, vol. 14. Arlington, VA: American Anthropological Association.

Whitten, Norman E., Jr. 1985. *Sicuanga Runa: The Other Side of Development in Amazonian Ecuador*. Urbana: University of Illinois Press.

World Bank. 2011. *Migration and Remittances Fact Book*. 2nd ed. Washington, DC: International Bank for Reconstruction and Development. http://siteresources.worldbank.org/INTLAC/Resources/Factbook2011-Ebook.pdf, accessed December 23, 2013.

Worster, Donald. 1977. *Nature's Economy: A History of Ecological Ideas*. Cambridge: Cambridge University Press.

Yashar, Deborah J. 2005. *Contesting Citizenship in Latin America: The Rise of Indigenous Movements and the Postliberal Challenge*. Cambridge: Cambridge University Press.

Zamosc, Leon. 1994. "Agrarian Protest and the Indian Movement in the Ecuadorian Highlands." *Latin American Research Review* 29, no. 3: 37–68.

Index